Rumours, Routes & Rapids

Finding your way in the Elk Valley

Rumours, Routes & Rapids

Finding your way in the Elk Valley

Bernie Palmer and Steve Short

Elk Valley Publishing

Fernie

Edited by B.S. Productions
Cover and interior photographs by Steve Short
Cover and interior design by B.S. Productions
Typeset by B.S. Productions, Fernie, B.C.

Printed and bound in Canada by Kromar Printing Ltd.

Canadian Cataloguing in Publication Data
Short, Steve.
      Rumours, routes and rapids

ISBN 0-9680036-0-5

1. Elk River Valley (East Kootenay, B.C.)--Guidebooks. 2. Hiking--British Columbia--Elk River Valley (East Kootenay)--Guidebooks. 3. Trails--British Columbia--Elk River Valley (East Kootenay)--Guidebooks. I. Palmer, Bernie. II. Title. GV199.44.C22E44 1995   917.11'65044 C95-910887-4

Disclaimer
      The author, editor, and publisher of *Rumours, Routes and Rapids* have used their best efforts to inform the reader as to the risks inherent in the outdoor activities described in this book. The level of expertise required to travel into largely unmarked, remote, and hazardous areas must be decided by the reader. If there is any doubt, please consult a guide who is familiar with the area to be explored. Topographical maps for the backcountry areas are a must. We take no responsibility for any loss or injury incurred by anyone using information contained in this book.

Dedicated to my mom, Arlene

She carried our first guidebook everywhere gathering memories and treasured moments. She loved to explore and was looking forward to this book, discovering the valley, and sharing it with her friends.

Rocky Mountain elk

Thanks to ...

All the enthusiastic locals who dedicated their time and energy providing details of routes. These locals are the 'route checkers' you will find at the beginning of most of the route entries. Lee-Anne Walker for her database, and the research time it saved us. Our publishing group for their enthusiasm, ideas and support, with special thanks to Gordon Zombrowski for working closely with us and keeping us on track.

A special thank you to Pat Gilmar for sharing his knowledge of the Elk Valley. Pat's route descriptions were always a challenge as he invariably started with "where not to go". We think that Pat is responsible for many of the rumours of routes in the valley. While most people hike a prescribed route, Pat on the other hand is like the Duracell rabbit. He keeps going and going until he's either lost or discovers a new route. These new routes are usually loop connectors between existing routes, a more appealing way of traveling than retracing your steps. In describing these routes in the book we've left some of them as options or a rumour for the more experienced hiker capable of mapreading and routefinding to investigate. We threatened Pat with putting his phone number in this book for people to call if looking for a guide, but at the last minute decided to be nice. (He is, however, in the phone book!)

Jack McKay, another route checker and our companion hiker deserves a special mention as well. Jack has more energy than most people do, but unlike Pat, discovers practically nothing along the way as he is usually going too fast. He does notice bears however, and is a most entertaining hiking companion.

Glenn Davis, his jeep, enthusiasm and all his outdoor toys enabled us to get to trailheads with ease, raft the river and have a lot of fun along the way.

Jim Drozduc of Canadian Helicopters for providing air time with the biggest toy of all for our reconnaissance.

Finally, a thank you to the City of Fernie and the districts of Sparwood and Elkford for helping sponsor the production of this book.

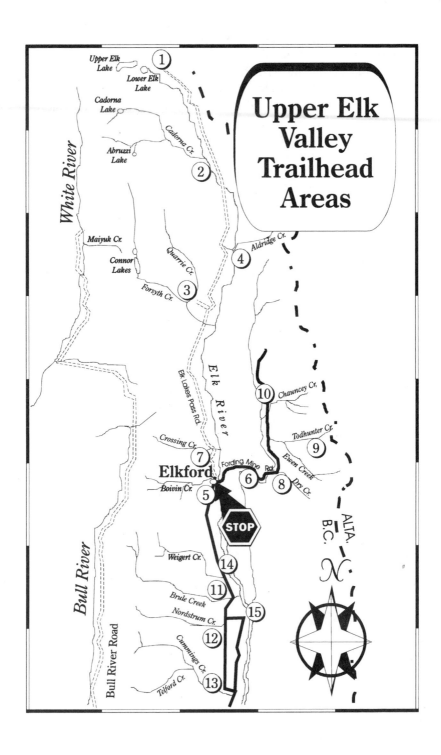

Rumours, Routes and Rapids

We heard the local rumours of the outdoor adventure to be had in the Elk Valley and decided to investigate. We discovered some trails, lots of routes and even more rumours that didn't always pan out. Often the directions were along the lines of, "Go up the old dirt road where Bud Walter's trapline used to be until you pass that big stand of birch they cut down a couple of years ago. Last week there was a dead skunk just off to the side of the road in the ditch just a little ways before the trail starts but you can't see it 'cause the road washed out and there aren't any berries up there anyway since the forest grew up, so I don't think you want to go there anyway." Yet no matter how convoluted the directions, they all led to memorable surprises and unbelievable scenery.

With help from many locals we chose trips that would give the best representation for all levels of fitness and experience. From casual walks to strenuous backpacking ordeals, back-country road biking to single track mountain biking, gentle float trips to white water adventure. In all, we found 33 trip entries covering 77 routes and 10 paddling sections considered by many to be Elk Valley's best.

The wilderness of the Elk Valley is an invitation to anyone to explore, discover, and appreciate the importance of keeping it intact. Our book provides a glimpse of what the valley has to offer, you'll discover much more on your journeys. Enjoy the experience of these trips and the adventure of finding your own discoveries along the way. We did, and found many surprises, inspiration, and indelible memories.

Steve Short and Bernie Palmer - Fernie, B.C., October, 1995

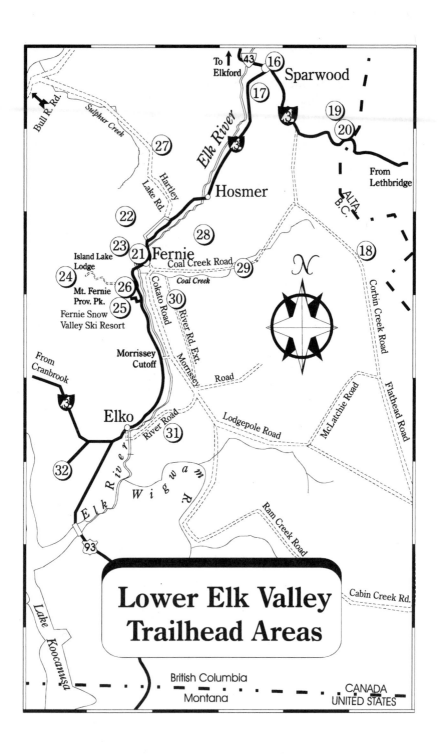

Lower Elk Valley
Trailhead Areas

Elk Valley

The Elk Valley was one of the last areas of the southern portion of the Rocky Mountains to be explored. Michael Phillips and John Collins discovered the Crowsnest Pass in 1873. They crossed into Alberta after prospecting for gold in the headwaters of the Elk River and Michel Creek. Their discoveries of coal were of little interest at the time. Twenty years later a growing western Canadian population and railway development made Elk Valley coal valuable. The development of the coal fields led to the founding of Fernie, followed by Sparwood and, most recently, Elkford.

Location and Access

The Elk Valley is located in the extreme southeastern corner of British Columbia. The valley is accessed from east and west by Crowsnest Highway #3 and Highway 93 from the south. Travelers who stop in the valley are invariably taken by the area's beauty, the rich wildlife and the friendly people who reside here.

Much of the backcountry is accessible with four-wheel-drive vehicles on industrial roads, many of which are still in use and require cautious driving. Huge trucks rule the road and travel at great speeds. On backcountry roads there are no services: ensure you have a full tank of gas, spare tire, repair tools, and plenty of windshield washer fluid.

Information Services and Tips

This book is not designed to give lessons in wilderness survival. We assume the reader venturing into the wilderness already has basic outdoor skills.

All routes in the Elk Valley can be found on two topographical maps - NTS 1:250 000 82G, and NTS 1:250 000 82J. We recommend the more detailed 1:50 000 series for routes requiring navigation or routefinding.

Remember to leave only footprints and take nothing with you but photos and memories. Although this area is not in a park and does not have the regulations of a park, it is home to many. Wildflowers are precious and are best left behind to grow and spread their beauty. Three Travel Infocentres, in Fernie, Sparwood and Elkford, serve the valley. Contact addresses and phone numbers are listed in the back of this book. You'll also find a resource listing for commercial outdoor recreation suppliers in the area.

Accommodations and Camping

You'll find accommodations to suit every kind of traveler in the Elk Valley. Accommodations available in the area are listed under 'Resources' in the back of the book.

Please be aware when camping that fire is a serious threat throughout B.C. in the summer. Ensure that campfires are completely extinguished before you go to bed or leave a campsite for any length of time. In case of fire dial "0" and ask for Zenith 5555 or 1-800-663-5555

Those clear, cool, bubbling streams, so common in the valley are an inviting thirst quencher. Unfortunately, in the backcountry there is always the risk of Giardia lamblia - an intestinal parasite that causes giardiasis a.k.a. "beaver fever." Treatment is available but to be safe it's best to carry your own water or take measures to purify the water. Don't risk getting Giardia - we've been there - done that, and it's not fun.

Climate, Flora and Fauna

Weather in the Elk Valley is typical mountain weather. It can change without much warning: make sure you can protect yourself from the sun, wind, rain, and cold. A common saying in the area is "If you don't like the weather wait five minutes, it'll change". Trouble is, it might get worse so be prepared.

The Elk Valley is part of the interior Cedar - Hemlock zone. This zone has the widest variety of coniferous tree species of any zone in the province. Both moisture-loving species such as western red cedar to dry-habitat species such as larch are found in the valley.

In addition to the usual species of wildflowers the Elk Valley is home to delicate and rare species such as beargrass which blooms only once per decade and calypso orchids. Insect pests are no worse here than anywhere else in the province. Ticks however, can be a problem in spring and early summer where herds of large animals live, hence most of the Elk Valley. Use insect repellent and if bitten, make sure you remove the entire "critter," including mouth parts which can carry disease. This region is well known on an international scale as excellent wildlife habitat. You can see deer, moose, elk, bears, goats, Rocky Mountain sheep, cougars, coyotes and smaller animals such as porcupines and beavers. Loons, grebes, wood ducks, golden and bald eagles, rosy finches and calliope hummingbirds are just a few of the birds found in the valley.

Extreme Caution: The most fearful of animals likely to be encountered, especially in wilderness areas, are bears. The Elk Valley is home to a large population of both grizzly and black bears. **All trips require bear awareness!**

Bears can attack when startled, especially if they are feeding or resting with cubs. People cause conflicts with bears by approaching them too closely, offering them food, attempting to drive them off, or trying to save apparently orphaned cubs.

Avoid bears by staying away from areas they are likely to be. They frequent alpine areas early in summer, feeding on marmots and fresh shoots of plants. Later in the season they're found near berries. During spawning season they inhabit river valleys. However - bears don't always follow these rules, so expect to find them everywhere.

Use a flashlight at night when camping and hang food in trees, well away from the campsite. Don't cook in or near your tent and don't leave garbage around. You may wish to consider carrying bear bangers, or chemical repellents. These should be available at outdoor stores.

If you see a bear at a distance, detour around it or wait until it leaves the area before continuing your journey. Avoid making the animal feel threatened - always leave an

Grizzly

escape route for the bear. If you encounter a bear at close quarters, slowly back away while talking to it calmly. This sometimes can alleviate any sense of threat to the bear, and may help you avoid panic. Backing away allows you to watch for aggressive behavior: snapping of jaws, making a woofing sound, or lowering its head with the ears pinned back. If there's a climbable tree slowly move toward it and climb as high as possible. Most adult grizzlies cannot climb trees but young grizzlies and black bears can.

If none of this works and you are attacked by a bear there are some things to consider. If attacked by a black bear, playing dead seldom works. It's considered better to try intimidating the bear by making noise or swinging large sticks. If attacked by a grizzly, curling up protecting your face, neck and stomach sometimes works. Leave your pack on for protection. Don't move until you are sure the bear has gone, even if he cuffs you a bit. With grizzlies, fighting back usually makes them angry, but as they're unpredictable, it might persuade one to leave you alone. There are no guaranteed methods when dealing with bears.

Bear awareness cannot be over-emphasized in the Elk Valley. Compared with most areas, the Elk Valley is crawling with them and hardly a day goes by without some mention of bears. Residents are used to them and conflicts are relatively rare.

Please note that with the abundance of wildlife this area is also popular with hunters in the fall. When hiking during hunting season use extra caution and be sure to wear brightly-coloured clothing. Ask the locals for the areas most used by hunters. It is best to avoid these during the hunting season.

Explanation of symbols and ratings in trip descriptions:

Hiking   Biking

Hiking & Biking   Paddling

Hiking and Biking Ratings

Easy - no steep grades, suitable for families and those with little experience.

Moderate - up and down grades, suitable for those in average physical condition.

Strenuous - steep grades, technical, suitable for those in excellent physical condition.

Trail: Marked track that can be easily followed, usually well-packed with obstacles removed.

Route: Most often is just the course to follow to your destination. Usually not well-defined, sometimes along game trails, and sometimes requiring bushwhacking.

International River Classification

Grade I: Small and regular waves; passages clear; occasional obstructions like sandbars and bridge pilings.

Grade II: Rapids of medium difficulty; passages clear and wide with occasional boulder in stream.

Grade III: Waves numerous, high, irregular with rocks and narrow passages. Advance scouting usually required. Canoes will water ship, unless equipped with spray covers, will require frequent emptying.

Grade IV: Difficult long rapids, powerful irregular waves, large boulders; advance scouting mandatory. Suitable for expert paddlers in **closed** canoes and kayaks.

Grade V: Very difficult, long and violent rapids; large drops; steep gradient; advance scouting usually required, but difficult due to terrain. Suitable for expert paddlers in **closed** canoes and kayaks with professional leadership.

Grade VI: Difficulties of Grade V carried to extremes. Nearly impossible and very dangerous. Suitable for teams of expert paddlers in **closed** boats at favourable water levels and after careful study, with fully trained and experienced rescue teams in position.

1 Elk Lakes Provincial Park

Pristine lakes, waterfalls, and glacier views.

Elk Lakes Provincial Park and Recreation area is one of the prettiest, yet least visited, of the Rocky Mountain parks. Even in high tourist season it is not unusual to have the entire 17,325-hectare park to oneself.

The park is named for the two pretty lakes which, in turn, are named for the many elk that once inhabited the area. Natural lakes, waterfalls and meadows are backdropped by the jagged summits and remnant glaciers.

Lower Elk Lake

This area is an unrivaled destination for wildlife viewers. Elk, white-tailed deer and moose frequent the forests and clearings near the lakes. At the higher elevations mountain goat, Rocky Mountain bighorn sheep, grizzly or black bear occasionally make an appearance. Birds commonly seen include spruce grouse, Clark's nutcrackers and chickadees, while the lake areas attract a variety of transient waterfowl.

Access: Begin at the four-way stop in Elkford. Travel 47 kilometres north on the Elk Lakes Pass Road to the Elk River crossing at Weary Creek. Cross the river and continue 43 kilometres on the Kananaskis Powerline Road to the parking area for Elk Lakes Provincial Park. From the parking area take the walking path to park headquarters where current information is available during tourist season.

All camping in the park is on a walk-in basis. Car campers can choose from several B.C. Forest Service campsites along the road from Elkford.

Elk Lakes Provincial Park is also accessible to hikers from Alberta's Peter Lougheed Provincial Park by hiking over Elk Pass to Upper Elk Lake. This route travels a moderate seven kilometres from the trailhead to the Petain Campsite near Upper Elk Lake.

Petain Falls Trail

In addition to close-up views of the waterfall there are inspiring views of the glaciers and rugged peaks above.

From park headquarters an exceptionally beautiful trail leads to Petain Falls. This trail provides a fine introduction to the park. Many routes to more remote areas depart from this trail. In the 8 kilometres between park headquarters and the falls the trail gains 200 metres in elevation. It winds along both Lower and Upper Elk Lakes through sub-alpine forests, meadows and outwash plains. Most hikers can make the trip to the falls in 2 to 3 hours. The wilderness camp at upper Elk Lake is a good base for exploring the upper valleys.

Petain Basin

Hikers can access the high alpine terrain of Petain Basin from the Petain Falls Trail. When the falls come into view

Petain Falls

after you come out of the woods from Upper Elk Lake a faint trail branches off to the right. This is the route to Petain Basin. It ascends the east side of an avalanche chute before crossing to the west side at a small waterfall. The route continues up the west side of the chute before breaking away at rock cairns that mark the way to the basin. The strenuous four-kilometre route ends in the basin. Where open terrain offers easy routefinding through natural rock gardens with stunning vistas all around.

Fox Lake Loop

Route Checkers: Judy McMahon & Heinz Weixelbaum

Fox Lake Trail forms a circuit to Upper Elk Lake with the option of a side trip to Frozen Lake.

The trail to Fox Lake leaves the Petain Falls Trail just past park headquarters. It then travels to the B.C./Alberta boundary and skirts Fox Lake before rejoining the Petain Trail at Upper Elk Lake Campground. It makes an interesting alternate route to Petain Falls before looping back to park headquarters past both Elk Lakes. An additional twist to the hike is possible by taking the detour to Frozen Lake.

From park headquarters cross the bridge over the small creek then take the first trail to the right. Hike through boreal forest and open grassy meadows for four kilometres to the B.C./Alberta boundary. Keep your eyes open for wild strawberries along the way. At the boundary a large map gives directions to Fox Lake and Frozen Lake.

Continue to the left, following the boundary and within 200 metres you come to a fork in the trail. The first optional side trip of the Fox Lake Loop goes to Frozen Lake via this right fork. This side trip requires 1.5 to 2 hours return.

Frozen Lake is a worthy destination. Nestled in a basin surrounded by mountains and featuring a small glacier, this aqua green lake is spectacular. Watch for mountain goats on the ridges above the lake. Continue back the way you came to the Fox Lake Loop trail.

Take the left fork 1.5 kilometres to Fox Lake. This small lake provides good habitat for moose so stay alert along the trail. Continue hiking on the trail for another 2.5 kilometres to Upper Elk Lake. Here you have the option of heading left down the trail to park headquarters or going right to the Upper Elk Lake Campground and beyond to Petain Falls.

Several other occasionally-used routes exist in the park. These routes are unmaintained, requiring bushwhacking in places and routefinding throughout. Check with the ranger regarding plans for hiking these routes.

2 Cadorna Lake

Gorgeous lake in a cirque basin.

Cadorna Lake is breathtakingly set in a cirque basin surrounded by mountain peaks situated in Elk Lakes

Recreation Area. The route is often soggy and is heavily-used by hunters. We recommend hiking in July and August when it is a bit dryer and before hunting season begins.

Access: Travel 52.4 kilometres north on the Elk Lakes Pass Road from the four-way stop in Elkford. Turn off to your left. A faded sign with Bighorn Outfitters is posted in the trees. A wooden fence on both sides of the road should be seen a short distance down this road. The road winds down to the lodge for Elk Valley Bighorn Outfitters Ltd. Park here. Motorized traffic is prohibited beyond this point.

Cadorna Lake

From the parking area near the lodge the trail skirts the south end of Riverside Ridge until forking at the eight kilometre point. Take the right fork 14.4 kilometres northwest up Cadorna Creek valley to Cadorna Lake. This is a six to eight-hour hike, best done as an overnight. Note - there is a cabin belonging to the outfitter just beyond the right fork. This is private property so please respect it and do not use.

The trail is incredibly scenic along the valley (the natives referred to this as the "Valley in the Heart of the Mountains") with Riverside Ridge on your right the entire way. This rugged trail has sections of deadfalls making it more suitable for hiking than biking. Expect to have wet feet hiking through the valley in the summer.

Abruzzi Lake

Follow the directions to Cadorna Lake up the seismic trail to the fork at eight kilometres. The left fork ascends Abruzzi Creek to Abruzzi Lake. This trail is shorter, (four to six hours) and less rugged than the one to Cadorna Lake.

At the end of the seismic trail a route continues over the saddle known as "Pass in the Clouds." Historically this route was used by early natives to get to Driftwood Lake and the White River (Middle Fork). Nowadays it extends hiking options from the Abruzzi Lake area.

By hiking through "Pass in the Clouds" you can cross the Continental Divide and access a route up the White River to Sylvan Pass, then the Palliser River and on into Banff National Park. Another route possibility is to travel to North Kananaskis Pass and Peter Lougheed Provincial Park via Leroy Creek. These routes are major undertakings and require detailed planning by experienced backpackers using topo maps.

3 Connor Lakes

Moderate four-hour hike to emerald green lake surrounded by mountains and glaciers.

The Forsyth Creek Trail accesses scenic, 68,000-hectare Height of the Rockies Wilderness Area. This game rich area extends northwest through the Rocky Mountains along the Continental Divide from Connor Lakes to the Albert River. Established in 1987, it is the first Forest Service Wilderness Area in British Columbia.

Being adjacent to Banff National Park, Peter Lougheed Provincial Park, the Elk Lakes Recreation Area and Elk Lakes Provincial Park, it is an integral part of the largest block of protected wilderness in the southern Rockies.

A great variation of elevation characterizes the area. From the Palliser River at 1,300 metres to Mount Joffre at 3,449 metres, the altitude range includes both lush forests and permanent ice fields. High mountains dominate the scenic values of the area which has 26 peaks higher than 3,050 metres. With seven major mountain passes and distinct habitats, the area is able to support a variety of wildlife species.

Large animals such as elk, deer, grizzly, black bears, and bighorn sheep thrive in the area. Of special significance, it is home to one of the densest populations of mountain goats in the world. This area also has a rich human history. Many of the trails have been traced back to cultures of 8,000 years ago. More recently, it was on the route of both the Palliser expedition and the Overlanders. Nowadays visitors can access the natural landscapes from 15 points around the area's perimeter. Please note: There are no motorized vehicles nor aircraft allowed in the area.

Mountain goat

Hike the Forsyth Creek area and you will be rewarded by a sense of being further into the backcountry than you really are. Just a moderate four-hour hike from the parking area at the trailhead brings you to superb scenery, access to Connor Lakes, Height-of-the-Rockies Wilderness Area, and routes to Elk Lakes Provincial Park.

Access: Starting at the four-way stop in Elkford drive 28.7 kilometres north on Elk Lakes Pass Road to the two brown pole signs for Connor Lakes Trail and Forsyth Creek. Turn left and travel 1.6 kilometres to a parking area at the B.C. Forest Service Recreation site overlooking Quarrie Creek. The area beyond is closed to motorized vehicles. A word of warning: Other vehicles parked at the trailhead when we were there were trussed up in wire mesh like a maximum security prison. There might be tire-chomping porcupines here.

Connor Lakes

From the parking area at Quarrie Creek to Connor Lakes return is 25 kilometres. This makes for a rather long day-hike and leaves little time for exploring the area around the lakes. A better alternative would be to backpack three to four hours prepared to stay overnight.

The trail begins at Quarrie Creek below the parking area for the Forestry Recreation Site. At the creek take the trail down to the left through the bush to a footbridge across the creek. Once across head right, to the old seismic road that roughly parallels Forsyth Creek.

It's an easy grade and a beautiful walk along the road. Grasses have reclaimed the roadbed and a well-beaten centre tread is pleasant to follow. Several small creeks provide water along the way. You could bike this first section as an option if doing it as a day trip.

The road ends at the old drill rig site clearing and becomes a trail heading north into the forest. The well-worn tread leads uphill briefly before winding down toward Forsyth Creek. It forks twice before reaching the creek - take the right fork both times.

Cross the creek on the footbridge. There is a second creek crossing just before a long uphill section. At the top of the hill the trail levels out paralleling the creek canyon but remaining out of sight of the raging waters. It descends to the shore of Connor Lake. Here hikers are rewarded with fabulous views of the lake and the Abruzzi Glacier beyond. The trail to the cabin goes around the west side of the lake.

Note: There may be three small aluminum skiffs at the south end of the lake. These provide the option of paddling

Abruzzi Glacier above Connor Lakes

the lake to the cabin but it takes about the same time as hiking. Fishermen use these boats more than hikers do and they could be left at either end of the lake. The primitive paddles and lack of life preservers makes traveling the lake a risky proposition. Wind can come up suddenly on narrow mountain lakes like this one and it might be difficult to get these unwieldy craft to safety in a hurry.

The size of the lake is deceiving and it is still an hour's hike to the cabin at the north end. Just before the end of the lake the trail forks. Take the right fork leading down and across a footbridge. Two more minutes of walking along the lakeshore brings you to the cabin.

The forestry cabin at the north end of the lake is available to the public free of charge on a first-come, first-served basis. It has a good stove, firewood and bunks for four adults or six close friends. Please respect it by cleaning up your mess. Officially the cabin belongs to the B.C. Forest Service. In reality, the packrats run the place. We can vouch for the fact that these little critters can make sleep difficult, if not impossible. Because of this we strongly advise coming to Connor Lakes prepared to camp out.

From the cabin you can hike upstream along the creek to the second small lake or take the trail directly behind the cabin for five minutes to the third lake and fantastic views of Abruzzi Glacier.

White River/Palliser River Route

Rugged hikers with routefinding skills and topo maps can cross the Continental Divide and continue to the White River. At the fork in the trail near the end of the first lake take the left fork rather than the right which goes to the cabin. The trail climbs steeply to the Continental Divide before descending along Maiyuk Creek for seven kilometres to the White River.

A horse trail goes 32.5 kilometres up the White River Valley through Sylvan Pass to the Palliser River. By continuing 20 kilometres up the Palliser River hikers can reach Banff National Park via Palliser Pass.

Offshoot branches of the trail lead to Tipperary Lake or to North Kananaskis Pass, via Leroy Creek.

4 Aldridge Creek

Moderate nine-hour hike or difficult seven-hour bike.

Best done as a mountain biking trip, the Aldridge Creek route offers views of the Burning Coal Seam on the south side of the valley and beyond into Alberta's Old Man River country.

Access: Drive the Elk Lakes Pass Road 39.4 kilometres north from the four-way stop in Elkford to the Aldridge Creek Road turnoff. Turn right, travel down to the river and park at the recreation site campground. Here you must ford the river to access the Aldridge Creek Road which is closed to motorized vehicles. Those not wanting to get wet travel another 7.3 kilometres on the Elk Lakes Pass Road to a fork. Take the right fork back to Aldridge Creek Road on the east side of the river.

Route: Follow the cart track along Aldridge Creek. Take the first right fork then the next left fork to Fording River Pass.

5 Elkford Environs

Many easy to moderate trails around Elkford townsite.

Located on Highway 43, 35 kilometres north of Sparwood, the small town of Elkford has limited services for the traveler. You will find gas, vehicle repairs and groceries, but don't expect to outfit yourself completely for a backwoods sojourn.

Elkford bills itself as the 'Wilderness Capital of B.C.' It certainly lives up to this claim and is becoming better known every year as a major destination for wilderness enthusiasts. Fortunately, you don't need to travel into the wilderness to enjoy the area. There are several easy to moderate trails in and around Elkford suitable for outings of half a day or less.

Elkford Recreational Access Trails

There are numerous easy bike trails skirting the perimeter of Elkford. These trails are great for those looking for short easy mountain biking within Elkford. These trails travel through fields, forests, alongside streams and to view points. They are accessible from various locations. Watch for red wooden signs indicating access points.

Bare Hill Lookout

This is a one-kilometre, self-guided interpretive trail leading up to a panoramic view of Elkford and the surrounding mountains. Pick up a self-guiding brochure at the Elkford Infocentre before taking this trail to make the trip a little more interesting.

From the four-way stop on Highway 43 turn left onto Alpine Way then right on Fording Drive before turning left on Corbin Drive. Follow Corbin Drive all the way to the playground at the junction with Galbraith Drive. The trail starts at the playground.

Mountain & River Trails

These two connecting trails are perfect for easy mountain biking or hiking. Beautiful subalpine forest and peaceful streamside sections are highlighted by great views of the Elk Valley. From the four-way stop turn left on Alpine Way, then right on Fording Drive and left on Natal Road. Follow Natal Road to the Wapiti Ski Hill parking lot. The Mountain Trail starts from the northwest corner of this parking lot. The Mountain Trail is a moderate two-hour hike one way to the footbridge crossing of the Elk River. The area at this crossing is known as Round Prairie. Once across the river you connect with the River Trail. You can either hike back the way you came, to the Wapiti Ski Hill parking lot, or continue on River Trail.

The River Trail can be accessed from the other side of Elkford. At the four-way stop in Elkford turn right off Highway 43, cross the bridge over the Elk River and immediately turn left onto a gravel road. Drive 2.4 kilometres to the powerline crossing. The trailhead is on the left 50 metres beyond the powerline. Look high in the trees and you should see a trailhead sign.

The trail winds approximately four kilometres to the bridge at Round Prairie where it connects with the Mountain Trail. The River Trail follows bends of the Elk River. Although this is an easy one-hour hike for most people, unstable banks and washout areas occur throughout presenting some safety risks. Caution at all times is advised.

Boivin Creek Interpretive Trail

This trail is an easy walk providing wildlife viewing, wildflowers and birding opportunities. A habitat enhancement project in 1992 and 1993 included seedling and tree planting. Interpretive panels, benches and picnic tables are further enhancements planned at the time of printing this book.

The trail begins at the bridge crossing on Fording Drive. The 1.2-kilometre interpretive loop follows a wide trail

Koko Claims (Crossing Creek)

along Boivin Creek. One footbridge crosses the creek along the trail. Watch the creek bed for a small slate-gray bird a little bigger than a sparrow. If it is doing little knee bends, then diving into the rushing waters, it is probably a Rocky Mountain dipper. These fascinating little birds cling to the bottoms of rushing creeks catching aquatic insects even in mid-winter. They are commonly seen from this trail.

Boivin Creek South Fork

Route Checker: Brian Spreadbury

This is a trip for energetic hikers or mountain bikers. From the four-way stop turn left on Alpine Way, then right on Fording Drive and left on Natal Road to the end of the pavement and park near a wide spot on a bend in the road near an open gate.

Start up the Boivin Creek drainage by following the road or the powerline which heads south briefly then turns west. Watch for moose along this section. Approximately three kilometres up the road the creek forks. The west fork goes into the base of Mt. Hadiken on a little-used trail which gets progressively rougher. Some very rugged bikers have even continued to Mt. Hadiken Pass and over to Crossing Creek following horse trails.

Stay on the main road along the south fork, known to old-timers as Wildcat Creek. Approximately seven kilometres from the trailhead (the kilometre markings along the road are wrong) you encounter a cabin next to the road. The future of this cabin is tentative as no permit was acquired to build it. Along this section watch the avalanche chutes on the other side of the creek on Profile Mountain during high snowfall years. Avalanches occasionally make it all the way across the creek, hitting the road.

About 400 metres past the cabin the road forks. Take the right fork which steepens considerably for 2.3 kilometres to its end at an old sawmill site. Look for an old seismic line which heads off the south end of the sawmill site directly toward a huge slump block at the base of Phillips Peak.

Follow it for about one kilometre to the base of the peak. This is a good place for late summer huckleberries. At the base of Phillips Peak you have two options. The first option angles off to the left about 300 metres up a steep slope to an ephemeral lake. Depending on the time of year there may or may not be water in it. Immediately above the lake and east of the turret on Phillips Peak there is a saddle. Rumour has it hardy hikers have continued over this saddle into Weigert Creek then out to Highway 43. Treacherous slab conditions often exist early in the spring so be wary.

The second option angles to the right along the base of the scree for about 1.2 kilometres. You break out of the timber into an alpine meadow at the base of the permanent snow field on the northwest face of Phillips Peak.

Hornaday and company camped in this meadow during an expedition funded by the Smithsonian Institute to collect large animal specimens back in 1905. Large animals still roam here today, including grizzlies. If you camp in the area be sure to bear-proof your camp. People camping at this site have had grizzlies try to get at their packs which were hung up in the adjoining timber.

By ascending the ridge to the west you can look into the Bull River drainage.

Wapiti Mountain

This is a difficult five-hour hike to the top of the Elkford ski hill. The summit of the Elkford Ski Hill offers panoramic views of the valley, alpine meadows and wildlife viewing opportunities.

From the four-way stop turn left on Alpine Way, then right on Fording Drive and left on Natal Road. Follow Natal Road to the Wapiti Ski Hill parking lot. Hike up the main ski run to the top right corner of the ski hill. There is no developed trail from here so you have to find your own way to the top. Traverse north to the divide area between the two main peaks, then hike up to the summit.

6 Forest, Falls & Lakes Trail

Easy interpretive trails for the entire family.

Of all the trails close to Elkford, the Forest, Falls and Lakes Trails are the best developed, featuring comfortable grades, excellent directional and interpretive signs, and the additional treat of views over the thundering cascades of Josephine Falls. Intersecting loops suitable for family hiking or biking offer interesting alternative routes.

Spending a sunny weekend afternoon exploring the Forest, Falls and Lakes Trails is an excellent family activity.

The forest section is a cool, easy walk with benches and interpretive signs along the way. The trail meanders past colourful patches of mosses and wildflowers. Even in mid-summer you can find a wide variety of flowers such as twinflowers, dwarf dogwood, paintbrush, bluebells and more.

The marshy areas buzz with colourful dragon flies in pursuit of mosquitoes. Well-built footbridges cross moist areas and the tiny lakes are alive in spring with ducks, kingfishers and red-winged blackbirds. Early morning visitors have a good chance of seeing big game animals.

Access: Turn right off Highway 43 at the four-way stop in Elkford. Travel up this road five kilometres, passing Greenhills Viewpoint to a right turn onto a gravel road. The parking area and map sign are visible as soon as you turn onto the gravel road.

Route: After consulting the map sign at the parking lot walk 2.3 kilometres through forest to the Josephine Falls overlook. Do not attempt to hike down the bank to the river below. The route down is not an established or recommended one. The slope is steep, slippery and loose rock tumbles down on anyone who might have already made the trip down. That's why there is a nice safe overlook. At

Josephine Falls

times the river is high and swift so a slip could end you up in a dunking at best.

From the overlook you can continue either to Lily Lake, Lost Lake, or do the entire loop. There are maps with distances posted at several places along the trail.

From Lost Lake you can take the trail back to Elkford rather than returning to the parking lot. It is a well-defined trail under a canopy of lodgepole pine.

To take this trail from Elkford to Lost lake turn right at the four-way stop and cross the bridge. Turn on the first road left across the bridge and park. The trail starts 350 metres north of the bridge to the right of the paved road. Gaining 250 metres the trail takes about 2 hours hiking or 1 hour biking to reach Lost Lake.

7 Koko Claims

Fast access to the Bull River

Route Checker: Gordon Zurowski

Bikers choose this route for fast and relatively easy access into the Bull River area. However, from mid-August on, locals seeking solitude and quiet avoid this area as it is also a haven for ATV users.

Access: From the four-way stop in Elkford travel north 5.6 kilometres to Round Prairie. The road up Crossing Creek (referred to as Koko Claims) starts on the west side of Highway 43.

Route: Take the road up the north side of Crossing Creek. The first 7 kilometres is moderate with the last 2.6 becoming strenuous ascending steadily to the pass and down to the Bull River drainage. Alpine meadows along the way highlight this route.

8 Dry Creek/Banner Mountain

Good wildlife viewing opportunities.

Route Checker: Brian Spreadbury

Warning - be aware that much of the land in the Fording Valley is private land (Dry Creek/Banner Mtn., Todhunter Creek and Castle Mtn./Chauncey Creek). By entering this area you may be risking injury due to mining operations. You might also face trespassing charges so make yourself aware of boundaries. Locals have advised that this valley is a prime hunting area and should be avoided during hunting season.

Access: From Elkford turn right at the four-way stop onto the Fording Mine Road. Travel 9.6 kilometres to the bridge over the Fording River. Proceed about 1.6 kilometres past the bridge and park at the north end of the reclaimed gravel pit on the west (left) side of the road immediately south of the Dry Creek crossing.

Route: Hike up the north side of Dry Creek for about four kilometres. The first couple of hundred meters is a bushwhack. You then cross a logging road and head up an exploration road through an old burn. Look for a poorly-marked jeep trail (cut by an overzealous sheep hunter from Elkford) on your left, just before a small tributary stream crossing. Follow this side drainage (jeep trail) for about 1.7 kilometres along a ridge to your left locally known as "Long Ridge." Then bushwhack through the fire-regenerated lodgepole pine to your left just prior to where the creek forks. Head for the open slopes to the northeast. Be on the look-out for sheep as this area is prime habitat. You can also climb 2,520 metre Mt. Banner (a subsidiary of Ewin Ridge).

9 Todhunter Creek

Difficult hike or mountain bike with good wildlife viewing opportunities.

Route Checker: Brian Spreadbury

This area features abundant wildlife, alpine meadows and many options for the hiker or biker.

Access: From Elkford turn right at the four-way stop onto the Fording Mine Road. Travel 14.3 kilometres and turn right onto a road that is the unsigned Todhunter Creek Road. The road crosses the railway tracks then forks. The road at this point is open to motorized traffic from June 16 to August 31. Todhunter Creek Road leading to Todhunter Lake and Mt. Gass is straight ahead, the right fork leading to Imperial Ridge.

Todhunter Lake/Mt. Gass

This option goes to either Todhunter Lake or Mt. Gass via the Todhunter Creek Road. You can hike, bike or sometimes drive up this road. About 3.7 kilometres from where it left the Fording Mine Road the road forks. Take the left fork for about 5.2 kilometres to another fork. Again take the left fork to climb the big talus pile known as Mt. Gass. Some bushwhacking is required at the top end of the logging blocks to get up onto Mt. Gass. The effort is well worth it, as the alpine meadows on Mt. Gass are spectacular in late July and early August.

To get to Todhunter Lake take the right fork instead of the left to Mt. Gass. Within about eight kilometres you will come to the top landing on the logging road system. At this point you will have been traveling for several kilometres through an old burn with all the snags cut down. From the top landing head north 200 to 300 metres to a rock outcrop. Ascend southeastward between the trees and rocks up a narrow meadow for about 500 metres.

There is no defined trail so routefinding skills are required. At the headwaters of Todhunter Creek are spectacular alpine meadows interspersed with stands of alpine larch which turn golden in fall. The slopes are covered with huckleberries in late summer. A good combination is to bike up to the headwaters of Todhunter Creek then hike into the alpine meadows.

Listen and watch for pikas, a rodent looking somewhat like a big hamster. They love rock piles and squeak loudly at passers-by.

Imperial Ridge

To take this option cross the railway tracks then take the right fork instead of heading up Todhunter Creek Road. Cross a bridge and proceed about 300 metres to the Ewin Creek Road junction. Turn left onto the Ewin Creek Road and look for Imperial Ridge to the northeast known by its exposed, grassy, southern slopes. This is an important winter range for bighorn sheep. Travel on Ewin Creek Road 1.8 kilometres to a fork in the road. Take the left fork crossing Ewin Creek before going north across the flats.

Just as the road starts to climb off the flats bushwhack a short distance off to your left and cross the creek. This brings you to the southeast corner of Imperial Ridge. Choose your own route from here to climb the ridge or head north along the base, climb the ridge to the north, drop into the east fork of Todhunter Creek and circumnavigate the ridge. Watch out for ticks in spring and early summer.

10 Chauncey Creek

Difficult hike or bike.

Route Checker: Brian Spreadbury

Alpine meadows, wildlife viewing, scenic camping and remote wilderness attract visitors to this area.

Access: At Elkford turn right at the four-way stop onto the Fording Mine Road. Travel 20 kilometres to where it crosses Chauncey Creek (also known as Smith Creek - named after Chauncey Smith). This area is closed to motorized recreation.

Chauncey Creek

Travel about 300 metres past the creek to a road turning off to the right. Take the road across the bridge over Chauncey Creek. About 400 metres up the road park at a junction with another road to your left.

Hike up the drainage and be prepared to cross the creek several times. Rough bridges may or may not be present. About three kilometres up the creek the valley floor broadens into subalpine meadows. Numerous destinations including small alpine lakes, are possible from here. Study a topo map to best explore the area and don't forget to bring the bear spray. This is prime grizzly country.

Castle Mountain

Continue along the Fording Road beyond Chauncey Creek. Over the next five kilometres are numerous places where you can pull off to the side of the road and begin hiking.

Old reclaimed exploration roads work their way up Castle Mountain which is on your right as you proceed north. Castle Mountain provides excellent opportunities for off-trail hiking and wildlife viewing. Elk, deer, and bighorn sheep can all be viewed if you are prepared to hike hard enough and high enough. Both the Fording Greenhills and Fording River operations are clearly visible to the west and north.

Be prepared to run into bears throughout the area and bring a topo map and compass with you as the west slope of

Castle Mountain has numerous pine-filled gullies that may confuse those not familiar with the area.

11 Brule Creek

Moderate to difficult hike with alpine meadows and wildlife viewing.

Route Checker: Bill Hanlon

Brule Creek area trails have some historical significance as well as recreational and scenic values. The Norboe/Brule Pass Trail was used as a trade route to the prairies by the First Nations. Hornaday Pass is named for W.T. Hornaday who captured large animals for the New York Zoological Park around the turn of the century. Brule Creek was called Avalanche Creek by Hornaday.

Access: From the junction of Highway 3 and 43 in Sparwood travel 19 kilometres north on Highway 43. Turn west on the marked gravel road (not suitable for vehicles) and travel 5.2 kilometres to a logging operation and gravel pit. At this point the road forks. Take the right fork and within 1.5 kilometres the road becomes a poorly-defined footpath.

Hornaday Pass Route

The rewarding scenic views come at the end of this long trek to the pass. It is approximately 10 kilometres (3 hours) through thick timber to Hornaday Pass from the beginning of the footpath. Vigilance is required as the main trail is subject to avalanches and there are many game trails to confuse you. The area is remote and routefinding skills are essential. The trail peters out just before the pass but the route is obvious.

Wildlife is plentiful along this route to the pass so keep your eyes open especially for bears. The pass itself is a good place to see goats and bighorn sheep. There is a cabin and unlimited tenting sites at the pass.

From here you can follow Norboe Creek 4.5 kilometres to the Bull River Road. The route down starts off steeply then becomes a gentle grade taking about two hours to the campsite on Norboe Creek.

Josephine & Big Lakes

On the route to Hornaday Pass where the footpath starts the path forks. Take the left fork here that leads up the drainage to Josephine Lake and Big Lake nestled between Mt. Roth and Mt. Terrion. This trail is difficult, requiring some bushwhacking.

12 Nordstrum Creek

Moderate four to six-hour biking round trip.

Route Checker: Bill Hanlon

Nordstrum Creek (Strong's Canyon) is a most scenic area and a wonderful bike trip, however as with Koko Claims, this area becomes overrun with ATV's after mid-August.

Access: From the junction of Highway 3 and 43 in Sparwood travel 19 kilometres north on Highway 43. Turn west on Brule Creek Road (not suitable for vehicles). A short distance in on this road a good road forks to the left. Follow this road down to Nordstrum Creek.

Route: There is a road all the way to the top of Nordstrum Creek. A very short route to open alpine and high ridges, requiring from two to four hours biking.

13 Cummings Creek

Moderate five to six hour biking round trip.

Route Checker: Bill Hanlon

This highly-rated mountain bike trail follows an old logging road. At the fork you can go right following Cummings Creek to access Mt. Frayn or left, following Telford Creek to access Mt. Washburn. Once again, in summer watch for the ATV's. Many new routes are being cut by these users.

Access: From the junction of Highway 3 and 43 take Highway 43 north towards Elkford 4.1 kilometres to the first left turn past the Lodgepole Trailer court. This road quickly becomes a cart track following the creek.

Cummings Creek

It is a steady, moderate climb of 17 kilometres along Cummings Creek. A cart track crosses Cummings (Wilson) Creek several times which is a consideration in high water. A few kilometres in, Telford Creek joins Cummings Creek. Cummings Creek Road continues along the right fork here.

Dew Drops on spider web

Telford Creek

Telford Creek continues along the left fork and is a shorter route providing access to an alpine cirque basin lake. You can walk to the base of the Mt. Washburn glacier from here. Mountaineers can gain access to Mt. Washburn from this location but some bushwhacking is required. This area may be logged in 1996. You might want to check this out before going.

14 Elk Valley Regional Park

About five kilometres of easy hiking and biking on unmarked but cut trails that crisscross the park.

For short hikes, a picnic or simply sitting watching the river go by, this quiet little park in the pines is a nice location to spend an hour or two.

If you're lucky you'll see herons stalking fish in the shallows of the river, while Kingfishers dive headlong after minnows from nine metres above the surface.

Access: From Sparwood at the junction of Highway 3 and 43 travel north on Highway 43 for 22 kilometres. The park is located on the right side of the Highway on the Weigert Creek drainage of the Elk River.

15 The Big Ranch

Easy walk or bike with hundreds of options through grassland and over rolling hills.

Referred to by locals as "The Big Ranch," this area is Class 1 winter range for elk and is closed to motorized traffic. The area is owned by the Nature Trust of B.C. and managed by the Sparwood & District Fish & Wildlife Association.

Access: At the junction of Highway 3 and 43, travel north on Highway 43 for 14.4 kilometres to the Lower Elk Valley Road. Turn right and travel 1.5 kilometres to where the road bends sharply to the right. The ranch is located east of the road beyond a sign indicating Grave Prairie.

Route: Bordered on the east by the Elk River this area offers 1000 acres of hiking and biking opportunities. Pick your own way. Caution is advised around the abundant wildlife.

16 Sparwood Environs

Numerous trail systems accessed from within the town of Sparwood.

Sparwood is the first B.C. town encountered after coming through the Crowsnest Pass from Alberta. It is located at the junction of Highway 3 and Highway 43 leading to Elkford. A full range of services is available to the traveler. Sparwood has a mall, grocery stores and limited outdoor supplies. Vehicle repairs and spare parts are readily available in Sparwood. The Infocentre is a good place to get current road and access information. It's the little tiny building beside the gigantic green truck.

Access: From the junction of Highway 3 and 43 take Highway 43 north towards Elkford 2.6 kilometres to the Sparwood Heights turn-off sign taking a left onto Arbutus Road. This road becomes Ponderosa Drive.

Sparwood Heights Trail

This easy two-hour hike begins in the Sparwood Heights subdivision. From Ponderosa Drive take the first left turn onto Cypress Drive, and park on the street 100 metres down Cypress.

The trail runs north off Cypress drive and ends on Valley View Drive. The easy-on-the-feet wood-chip trail meanders through a varied landscape of aspen, lodgepole pine, mature spruce and western larch along the banks of the Elk River. The diverse ecosystem offers expansive views, a variety of flora and birdwatching opportunities. Walk back from Valley View Drive along Ponderosa Drive to Cypress Drive then through Cypress Park back to your vehicle.

Matevick's Draw

Difficult five-hour hike to complete a loop with good views of the valley from the top. You hike through willows and alders then some windfall and spruce. Keep a lookout for ruffed grouse, elk and black bear. This trail is covered in snow until the middle of June.

Continue on Ponderosa Drive to its end. Take Sycamore Road to the right toward the ski hill. Continue on this road until you cross under the power lines where you can pull over and park. The trail enters the forest on the west side of the road about 15 meters from the road.

The trail through Matevick's Draw is four kilometres to the top of Sparwood Ridge. This is a horse trail, well-packed and wide for the first few kilometres. It then begins climbing into a slide area covered in willows following the valley floor. The trail gains about 600 metres in elevation crossing the gulch from one side to the other. Once on the flat landing of the ridge the trail ends. Either return the way you came or continue south along the ridge then descend Lladnar Creek.

17 Mountain Shadows

Easy two-hour hike, moderate one-hour bike.

Mountain Shadows Loop is a 4.7-kilometre trail system that winds through a mixed forest. Western larch needles carpet the trail, and Calypso orchids can be spotted in the shady, moist soil alongside the trail. These orchids are becoming very rare. Do not pick or try to transfer them to your garden as they won't grow. They require very specific soil and other environmental conditions, specific to where they are already growing. Watch for bears, of course, and the nuthatches and woodpeckers that also favour this area.

Access: This loop trail begins at the Mountain Shadows campground or at the entrance to the Sparwood Golf Course. To access the trail from Mountain Shadows campground travel one kilometre west from the junction of Highway 3 and 43 at Sparwood. Turn left following the signs to the campground. To access the trail from the golf course take the turnoff to the golf course across from the Travel Infocentre on Highway 3. The trailhead is up the golf course road 250 metres on the right.

18 Andy Good Creek

An easy to moderate seven-kilometre hike or bike with wildlife viewing.

This is an area rich in wildlife, offering opportunities to see elk, mule and whitetail deer, moose and bears along the babbling creek. Those a bit more adventurous can continue at the end of this hike to the caves and plateau. Please respect the private property and cabins along the route. Note: Route crisscrosses the creek which could be difficult when the water is high. In fact, one of our route checkers was once stranded here by a flash flood so keep a close eye on the weather.

Access: From Sparwood at the junction of Highway 3 and 43 travel east on Highway 3 for 10.8 kilometres. Turn south toward the Coal Mountain Operation on Corbin Creek Road and travel 21 kilometres to a cart track on your left just before the railroad tracks. You can park on the right just past the tracks. The cart track meets up with Andy Good Creek a bit further upstream.

Andy Good Creek

Route Checker: Gord Henning

The seven-kilometre cart track can be hiked, biked, or at times, driven with a four-wheel drive. It becomes rougher the farther along the trail you get. Proceed 250 metres on the cart track to a fork, taking the uphill left fork and thereafter every right fork. The trail climbs into a basin, crossing the creek several times before ending at a thick spruce stand.

From the stand of spruce hikers with routefinding skills and a topo map can continue up to a karst plateau on a rough trail to access Gargantua, Camp and Cleft caves. This section to the caves will take approximately five hours.

Please note: Cave exploration is hazardous requiring specialized skills and extensive spelunking experience. If you don't know what spelunking means then you probably shouldn't be going into big caves without experienced partners.

There is an easier access to the caves. Unfortunately, it is from the Alberta side.

Flathead Pass

Route Checker: Pat Gilmar

Rumour has it you can reach spectacular views of Alberta, high basins, and the front ranges of the Rocky Mountains from the pass.

Continue past Andy Good Creek for about nine kilometres climbing up to Flathead Pass. Watch for a cart track heading off to your left just before the crest of Flathead Pass. The road only goes in about 50 metres before a locked gate bars further access.

From here you hike a cart track about 7.5 kilometres gaining about 750 vertical metres to a saddle in the Flathead Range. Retrace your route for the return.

19 Alexander Creek

Moderate eight-hour hike or six-hour bike.

Highly recommended for bikes to Deadman Pass. It's long and strenuous but not technically difficult and "not killer," in the words of a local biker.

Access: From Sparwood at the junction of Highway 3 and 43 travel 16.5 kilometres east on Highway 3 to the weigh scale. Cross the cattleguard 100 metres west of the weigh scale on Highway 3 onto the road heading north up the valley. Just beyond the cattleguard the road forks but comes together again so it doesn't matter which fork you take. This is a four-wheel-drive road and open to vehicles so bikers must exercise caution. The road is located on Crestbrook Forest Industries property so please respect the property and obey the rules.

Alexander Creek/Deadman Pass

From the start of the four-wheel drive road to Deadman Pass turnoff is 8.7 kilometres. The turnoff to Deadman Pass is just after a cattleguard and just before a bridge. The road leading to Deadman Pass heads off to the right. A strenuous climb leads to the pass, then you can travel across the

Alberta border, and beyond into the Allison Creek Recreation Area.

Those wanting a loop route can continue north along the ridge from Deadman Pass to Allison Peak and over to Racehorse Pass. The four-wheel-drive road leading down from Racehorse Pass to Alexander Creek Road is passable for hiking but not biking since the flood of 1995.

Upper Alexander Creek Valley

Rumour has it that rather than turning off to Deadman Pass you can continue along Alexander Creek to the Alexander Creek Forest Service Campgrounds. From here you can explore the upper valley of Alexander Creek. Cutline trails lead to basins such as Goat, Charlie's, Fedorek, Sheep and Nine Mile, as well as Racehorse Pass on the west-facing slopes of the Continental Divide.

At the end of the valley the road climbs 2,250 metres over the ridge known by the locals as 'the Crown', into the Grave Creek Valley. This route over 'the Crown', however, is "hard core" mountain biking.

On the north side of the ridge the road drops into the Grave Lake Campground.

20 Phillipps Pass

Easy 1 to 1.5 hour hike to great views of the valley and Alberta. The more energetic can climb Mt. Tecumseh.

Follow the footsteps of Michael Phillips, the first white man to discover the Crowsnest Pass. In 1872 he was prospecting from west to east when he discovered the route, the only pass in the Rockies discovered from the west. He discovered the pass while following elk trails and river banks, knowing, when his party found buffalo signs that they had come through a pass without crossing over any mountains.

Beargrass

History books spell his last name "Phillips," however modern maps spell this name as "Phillipps" when referring to Phillipps Pass. We have used the history book spelling when referring to Michael Phillips and modern map spelling when referring to Phillipps Peak.

There are two routes through the Crowsnest Pass. One route is the one Highway 3 now follows. The other route (Phillipps Pass) is just north of the highway. During prohibition rum runners used this route to evade the Alberta Provincial Police checkstops on Highway 3.

Access: From Sparwood at the junction of Highway 3 and 43, travel 17.6 kilometres east on Highway 3 to the Crowsnest Rest Area on your left.

Route: Follow a gravel road that circles behind the picnic/parking area to a parking area. Directly east of the parking area is the Alberta Natural Gas pipeline road. Follow this road east taking the right fork up to its first high point where you can look down the valley and into Alberta. This is a short hike taking about 45 minutes resulting in wonderful mountain panoramas on both sides.

Once at this first high point you have the option of following the road down to Phillipps Lake, around the lake and back up to a point just south and a bit higher than where you are now at this first high point, then continuing up to the Microwave Tower. This option to the lake and back up requires an additional 45 minutes and entails regaining elevation back up from the lake.

The second option is shorter and doesn't lose any elevation. Look for a small white post to your right where the road levels off at the top of this first high point. You can hike up a short distance from the post through open forest to where the road winds up from the lake. Once here you can continue on the gasline road or take the ridgeline along Crowsnest Ridge to the Microwave Tower. Whatever route you take to the tower the views are great and you feel far removed from the traffic speeding through Crowsnest Pass on Highway 3 below.

21 Fernie Environs

Easy hike or bike following the Elk River and skirting Fernie.

Fernie is a coal-town-turned-ski-town rapidly turning outdoor recreation Mecca. Although officially a city, it is a friendly little mountain town. Many of the residents have come here to escape the city lifestyle, exchanging it for one involving more leisure time and healthy activities. Because of the ski resort and the fabulous terrain so well suited to backcountry recreation, there are several good outdoor shops catering to the modern biker, hiker and skier. Fernie is probably the best town in the Elk Valley to find recreation gear and outfit yourself for backcountry muscle-powered travel.

Fernie's setting is spectacular. It lies nestled at 1,020 metres in the mountains beside the beautiful Elk River. The Lizard Range, Three Sisters and Mt. Hosmer areas offer excellent hiking and biking opportunities within sight of town. Fernie's history has included both fire and flooding. Most recently in June of 1995 when the Elk River flooded. The majority of the damage was to bridges, most of which had been repaired as this book went to press. It is best to check with the local Infocentre before heading far into the back country on logging or mining roads. A benefit for the back-country traveler seeking solitude is that some accesses are more difficult now than before the flood. (Lots of people still think we're under water so they aren't showing up at all.)

Note: There are two bridges on Highway 3 in Fernie. One is referred to as the "north bridge" and is on the highway heading toward Sparwood. The other is referred to as the "south bridge" and is on the highway heading toward the ski resort or Cranbrook.

Elk River Dike Trail

Route Checkers: Dave, Susan, Hannah & Emily Keiver

As an "in town" trail with an "away from it all" feel the dike trail is quite enjoyable.

A level, peaceful trail that allows you to walk or bike through the city without really feeling like you're in it. This beautiful, shale-track trail developed by the City of Fernie, starts at the north bridge on Highway 3, however it can be accessed from numerous points along the way. It runs along the river through town and ends at Mountain View Park which offers great views of the Lizard Range and Fernie Snow Valley Ski Resort. Along the way are park benches affording enjoyment of the views or the entertaining water fowl. This makes for a lovely evening walk or bike by the river.

Access: Although the trail starts at the north bridge, parking is not readily available. Those wishing to start at this end could park in the Annex subdivision or at a small parking area by the river on the north bank then walk back across the bridge to the dike.

Route: The first leg of the trail on bikes at a family pace takes 15 to 20 minutes and someone walking could take twice the time. The trail is a bit bumpy until you reach the Annex Park area where it's better-used and smoother. The Annex Park is a pleasant area of cottonwoods and open grassy areas where the kids can play.

There are alternate trails through the park with benches located at various places; good places to just sit and relax. The pond, formed by a diversion in the river, is used by many for swimming but more often you'll see ducks on it. Goldeneyes - black and white ducks with a white face patch and the brilliantly-coloured iridescent green wood ducks can sometimes also be seen. Noisy green-headed mallards are the most common as they are fed daily by local residents. Sometimes in the morning just as the light is hitting the tops of the Three Sisters, there are great blue herons fishing. This section concludes at the south bridge.

The second leg of the Dike Trail is also about 20 minutes biking and begins at the south bridge going to the north entrance of the airport subdivision where you cross over Coal Creek (there isn't an airport so there aren't any aircraft noises). This section winds through treed areas and then follows a road along the south bank of the Elk River.

Although it skirts the residential sections of the city there is still a feeling of solitude. Sometimes bald eagles perch on high cottonwoods and signs of beavers mark many of the streamside trees. At the end of the road a trail turns up Coal Creek for a short distance coming back out on a paved road. Cross the bridge here and turn immediately right after the bridge to continue to Mountain View Park.

The third leg of the Dike Trail follows the dike along the south side of Coal Creek beside the residential area. The trail takes you into Mountain View Park which offers places to rest along the river. At the south end of the park the trail brings you back into the airport subdivision. This leg requires about 15 minutes by bike. Once here you have the option of being picked up, traveling through the subdivision back to town, coming back via Cokato Road or retracing your route. Once back in town it's possible to connect to the heritage walking tour if you are interested in the turn of the century architecture.

22 Fairy Creek/Mt.Proctor

Difficult seven-hour hike with spectacular views.

Route Checker: Pat Gilmar

Although this is a demanding hike, the view is well worth the effort. This is a trip with something for everyone interested in natural history. The elevation gain showcases plant and animal biodiversity, with habitats from low elevation riparian woodlands to alpine flower meadows. Activities along the way include wildlife viewing opportunities and rockhounding for fossils. There are hazards, especially for the unwary. It is excellent bear habitat and the trail crosses several avalanche paths so caution should be exercised.

Fairy Creek Falls

Access: From Fernie follow Highway 3 east and take the first left turn immediately after the north bridge. Follow the road 400 metres to a turnoff to the right onto Fairy Creek Road. Continue north along Fairy Creek Road 800 metres going under the powerline and turning right just before the closed gate to park. Bypass the locked gate after reading the warnings. From the gate the trailhead is 200 metres up the road on the right. There is a sign indicating the trailhead for Fairy Creek.

Fairy Creek

The Fairy Creek portion of the trail is about one hour through mixed forest. Along the way huge stumps bear witness to the logging activities that once supported many of the earlier residents of Fernie. Twinberry and tiny blue violets garnish the mosses and lichens of the forest floor providing a pleasing diversion while you gain 260 vertical metres.

Note: A trail to the base of Fairy Creek starting from the Fernie Infocentre was in the making at the time of writing this book. Check with the Infocentre to see if this trail is accessible.

Mt. Proctor

The trail to Mt. Proctor is a continuation of the Fairy Creek Trail. It becomes the Mt. Proctor Trail where the Fairy Creek Trail bends sharply to the right heading uphill. The first section of the Mt. Proctor Trail continues its ascent through a trail overgrown with berry bushes prompting trail talk of past bear encounters. In this section experienced hikers tend to talk a little louder and finger their bear spray.

To gain the top of the ridge of Mt. Proctor (2,391 metres) takes about four hours for a hiker with a good fitness level. Along the way there are inspiring views of the Three Sisters, a classic Fernie area landmark. The views improve as the bushes thin toward the top of the ridge and the rugged south exposure of the Three Sisters looms imposingly on your left. From the top of the ridge there is a spectacular view over Fernie Mountain in the direction you came from, the town of Fernie far below and the peaks far to the southeast into the Flathead and beyond.

Remain attentive after the high of reaching the top wears off. Hikers must pay attention to the route as there is no trail on the ridge. Stay on the crest of the ridge, working your way south and then down the ridgeline back into the forest where you regain the trail. During the descent the views continue to enthrall almost all the way down until the powerline is reached. Turn right at the powerline, cross over the fence and follow the trail down to Fairy Creek. Cross the creek via a log and follow the road up to your vehicle. The entire route takes 7 to 10 hours. Keep a watchful eye on the weather as it can be confusing near the top in foggy conditions. Also be careful of the scree slopes - they often end in severe drops and sudden stops!

The city of Fernie as seen from the steep slopes of Mt. Fernie

23 Moccasin/ Mt. Fernie

Shortest route to a mountain top overlooking Fernie.
Extremely steep hike or bike.

Access: Travelling west, cross the south bridge at Rip 'N'
Richard's. Take the first right past the bridge onto Riverside
Road, then the first left onto Beach Street which becomes
Burma Road. Continue up Burma Road .5 kilometres to the
communications antennas on the uphill side of the road. The
trail begins on a deeply-rutted road immediately adjacent to
the dishes heading north.

Moccasin

The Moccasin (the sole-shaped clearing on Mt. Fernie's
south face) is a brutal uphill grade biking to the start of the
Mt. Fernie Trail, taking about one hour. There are excellent
views along the way of the ski resort and Lizard Range. The
trail starts as a deeply-rutted road then ascends the north
side of Mutz Creek. Within one kilometre the road crosses
under the powerline and then forks to the right directly up
toward Mt. Fernie. Ascending steadily it switchbacks only
five times before ending at a commanding view at the top of
the Moccasin. The top of the Moccasin has views good
enough to satisfy many who turn back here.

Mt. Fernie

The route from the top of the Moccasin to the top of the
ridge on Mt. Fernie follows a dry creek- bed and is steep and
straight, taking about one hour. This is a hiking trail only
and is not suitable for biking. The surface of this route up
the creek bed is hard and impenetrable to soft shoes. Wear
good hiking boots and prepare yourself for increasingly
steep grades all th way to the top. About halfway up a cable
assists the hiker to the top of the surprisingly narrow

ridgetop. The view from the ridgetops is directly over Fernie with Three Sisters, Mt. Proctor and Mt. Hosmer to the North and Morrissey Ridge south across the valley. The views are tremendous but the ridgetop is not as easy to negotiate as it might seem from below. The descent to the parking area from here takes about one hour.

Three Sisters and Mt. Proctor as seen from the top of Mt. Fernie

24 Island Lake

Numerous options for biking and hiking with great views, wildflower meadows, and wildlife viewing opportunities.

Access: The trails above Island Lake all begin at the Island Lake Lodge or from Cedar Valley Road leading up to the lodge. From the Fernie south bridge travel 2.3 kilometres west to the turnoff on the right for Fernie Provincial Park.

Travel one kilometre to the park and through to the end of the pavement. Here the Cedar Valley Road starts and continues eight kilometres to Island Lake Lodge. This road is dirt-packed and when wet a four-wheel-drive vehicle is recommended.

Island Lake Lodge Area

Skiers are familiar with the spectacular snowcat skiing at Island Lake. Many have yet to discover the world class summertime outdoor recreation opportunities. A tiny mountain lake set against the backdrop of the Lizard Range is accessible by road and provides a great starting point for hiking and biking in one of the most beautiful settings of the southern Rockies.

Biking the road to the lodge involves a lot of climbing but the trip is special as it climbs past old growth cedar giants 400 years old. Along the road glimpses of the rugged peaks are especially impressive in fall after the first dusting of snow. Sub-alpine larch forests gild the hills with golden hues. At the top you can enjoy the beautiful lake and mountain views or relax on the deck of the lodge.

Biking from Highway 3 to Island Lake Lodge return is 20 kilometres and takes 2 to 3 hours. The trip to the lodge is the first running stage of the Cedar Valley Old Growth Classic duathlon, held for the first time in the fall of 1995.

Island Lake Loop

There is an easy walking/biking trail partly on a snowcat road around the lake. The trail takes you through the forest crossing the outlet marshy area at the south end of the lake before looping back to the lodge. As a run this is the third stage of the Cedar Valley Old Growth Classic duathlon. Watch for the cow moose that calves on the lake's tiny island in spring. And always be bear aware at Island Lake. One party watched seven grizzlies fishing in the outlet creek in the spring.

Island Lake

Island Lake/Iron Pass/Bull River

Route Checker: Tom Soles

From Island Lake Lodge to the Bull River is a moderate three hours biking. There are great views along the entire trip. From the parking lot at Island Lake Lodge head back down the road to the first left (100 meters). Here a snowcat road starts down then crosses a creek. This road follows the powerline almost the entire way. Enjoy the downhill - it's the only one for the next hour or so. The snowcat road climbs up until you reach the Iron Pass summit at 1698 metres. Some say this is the best view in the area of the Bull River country.

From the pass you have a major, but short, arm-burning descent. Then the ride is full of ups and downs following East Iron Creek. There are six major creek crossings with the last being the most difficult. Wet feet are inevitable. There is a cabin along the way with a picnic table near the creek which is a good place to stop for lunch.

From the cabin the route continues down to the confluence of Iron Creek and the Bull River. You can either return to Island Lake the way you came or continue across the Bull River. If returning be prepared for about a 3.5 to 4-hour ride back. Ascending Iron Pass requires granny gear almost the entire way.

If continuing on, the first and only obstacle is getting across the river. Fording the river which is still waist-deep late in the summer can be difficult. Search upstream for a safe place to cross. Make sure the day chosen is warm enough to dry yourself off after fording, or waterproof a dry set of clothes for the descent to the inn.

Once across the river turn left on the Bull River Road. Travel beyond the dam 300 metres taking the right fork in the road down to the bridge crossing the Bull River Canyon. From the bridge to the Bull River Inn is 11.6 kilometres. It's probably best to shuttle vehicles from the inn as biking back to Fernie is a long ride.

Howling Coyote

Route Checker: Darcy Richardson

This intermediate two-hour bike ride takes riders through some of the valley's best scenery. This is the second stage, biking route of the Cedar Valley Old Growth Classic duathlon.

From Island Lake start on the same snowcat road as for the Iron Pass/Bull River route and continue to the Iron Pass summit.

Once on the summit go slow; it is tempting to let 'er rip but you might miss taking the proper route. Just past the summit on the downhill to the Bull River there is a sign indicating the road ahead is closed to motorized traffic. Just past the sign an old cart track heads off the road to your left, this is the route you want to take.

This old cart track is overgrown so take care watching for rocks and trail depressions. The cart track wraps around the back side of Mt. Baldy. The trail climbs to Baldy's Ridgeline traversing back and forth along the ridge gaining elevation the whole way. On the final switchback the whole Bull River country becomes visible. This is the place to stop, rest, and absorb the view as it is better here than at the very top of Mt. Baldy. You still have a 90-metre climb to the top.

From the top take the right fork heading down towards Island Lake and the valley below. If you go straight here you come to a dead end which gives a beautiful view of the Lizard Range and the valley floor. The only hitch is that you have to climb back up the trail to take the right fork and then start the downhill.

Warning: Bikers on the first portion of the downhill should watch for rocks on the trail, take time and savour all the effort you put into reaching the top. There are a few very steep sections on the downhill so remember - get that butt off the saddle, put it over the back tire and make sure your brakes are working at peak performance level. Once down on the valley floor stay left and the trail will take you to the Island Lake parking lot. Note: to make a real grunt (adding two hours to the trip) start from town instead of driving to the lodge.

Cabin Ridge Trail

Route Checkers: Pat Gilmar & Jack McKay

This route is a steep hike through old growth cedar forest (read stinging nettle, Devil's club and wasps) and through alpine meadows to spectacular views, wild rock gardens and the Thunder Meadows Cabin.

From Highway 3 at the turnoff for Fernie Provincial Park travel 6.5 kilometres to the trail-head sign for Cabin Ridge Trail on the left side of the road. There is a one or two car parking pullout space available.

The trail through the cedar forest is steep in places and directly uphill most of the way with just a few switchbacks (more like slight bends in the trail than switchbacks). Once through the forest, the trail becomes a route angling left, then climbs through rock gardens of penstemon, paintbrush and saxifrage through Cabin Bowl to the cabin. Once at the cabin you can return to Cedar Valley Road the way you came or continue southwest along the ridge to the Fernie High Trail. This route is described later as "Thunder Meadows to Fernie High Trail Connector Route."

Lower Elk Lake

Elk River north of Elkford

Elk River and Riverside Ridge

Connor Lake

Elk Valley above Elkford

Mt. Broadwood Nature Conservancy

Island Lake and Lizard Range

Elk Valley above Fernie

Old growth in the Cedar Valley

Lizard Lake/ Cabin Ridge Trail Loop

Route Checkers: Jack McKay & Pat Gilmar

From Highway 3 take the turnoff for Fernie Provincial Park and travel 3.3 kilometres to a left turn onto a dirt road. This leads to the parking area for the Lizard Lake Trail.

From the parking area cross Lizard Creek onto an old cart track. Take the right fork uphill and continue to the sign for Lizard Lake on the right side of the cart track. The trail starts off with a steep climb through forest with a few welcome views to stop, gawk and rest at. It continues onward and upward about 1.5 to 2 hours to a pretty alpine lake nestled in a grassy bowl with alpine meadows all around. This is a fabulous place to linger on a warm sunny day. Watch quietly and you could see moose around the lake or mountain goats on the ridge. Some end the hike here and return the way they came.

Lizard Lake

Those continuing ascend the Lizard Ridge from Lizard Lake. The trail up to the ridge has few switchbacks and fewer markers. To the very top of the ridge takes about another hour. Once on the ridge you have two options. You can hike along the ridge southwest to the Ski Resort via the 'Thunder Meadows to Fernie High Trail Connector Route' described in the next entry. Or you can continue along the ridge northwest to Thunder Meadows Cabin and down Cabin Bowl Trail to Cedar Valley Road. The following describes this latter route.

Traverse the ridge northwest to Thunder Meadows Cabin. This is a great ridge walk with a fantastic 360 degree panorama all the way to Orca Rock, a large outcrop on the Elk Valley side of the ridge. The cabin is visible on the west side of the ridge and just a ten-minute walk from Orca Rock. Follow the Cabin Ridge/Cabin Bowl Trail back down to Cedar Valley Road. Turn right on the road and follow it down about three kilometres to where you left your vehicle at the Lizard Lake trailhead. This loop takes about seven hours.

Hikers on the Connector Route

Thunder Meadows/Fernie High Trail Connector Route

Route Checker: Ian Henzie

This full day, moderate hike might be a good option for those overnighting at the Thunder Meadows cabin. This is another spectacular hike featuring ups and downs along the Lizard Range ridge with views of small lakes and the ski resort.

Access Thunder Meadows Cabin from the Cabin Ridge/Cabin Bowl Trail. Beginning from the cabin gain the ridge by hiking the slope to the east of the cabin. From the ridge there are great views of the Elk and Cedar valleys.

Hikers on Lizard Ridge

A steep pitch is encountered fairly quickly as you gain elevation on the ridge by hiking up what is referred to as "One Steep Mother." This section is made easier by staying on the right side of the ridge. Once at the top of "One Steep Mother" views of the surrounding mountains get better with a great view of Thunder Meadows and Lizard Lake. From here you drop into Liverwurst Pass, paying for the downhill with a big uphill on the other side of the pass to get back to the higher elevations on the ridge. Shortly after gaining back the elevation from Liverwurst Pass, Snake Ridge coming up from the east intersects the Lizard Range ridge. This intersection is the actual start of the Fernie High Traverse Trail which continues along the ridge to the ski resort.

Not only is this a beautiful route, but it also travels through some fabulous wild strawberry and huckleberry patches. Although best done as an overnight trip, the long Lizard Range ridge walk is made harder with overnight packs.

25 Snow Valley Ski Resort

Numerous options from easy to strenuous for biking or hiking.

Locally known as 'the ski hill', the Fernie Snow Valley resort area is cherished by skiers 'in the know' for its fabulous powder and friendly atmosphere during the 140 day ski season. The cleared runs, service roads and trails are used extensively in summer for biking and hiking to areas with some of the greatest panoramas of the Elk Valley near Fernie. During summer, access is made easier by chairlift rides up as far as the Bear's Den from which the alpine meadows can be reached in under an hour.

Access: Travel 5.3 kilometres west of Fernie from the south bridge on Highway 3 and take the turnoff right to the Fernie Snow Valley Ski Resort. Ascend the road 1.4 kilometres to the Griz Inn Parking Lot. Trails begin from here at the base of the ski hill.

The Quad Chair Ride

The chairlift taking you to the Bear's Den operates during July and August. It is an easy way to reach terrific views of the valley. It is also ideal for the handicapped and movement-impaired to reach mountain highs otherwise not accessible to them. From here you can walk or bike up to the alpine meadows above or down the ski runs or roads. You can also take the chair back down. Allow two hours for the ride up and down plus time to enjoy the view, fresh air, and mountain meadows.

Fernie High Trail

Route Checker: Linda Socher

This is the classic high route of the Fernie area with hiking, steep climbs, some scary sections and ridgewalking through subalpine forest. It is a demanding 8 to 10 hour loop. Once on the top above Snake Ridge you can hike to Thunder Meadows Cabin via the 'Thunder Meadows to Fernie High Trail Connector Route'.

Fernie High Trail goes the opposite direction along the ridge. Hike up Snake Ridge then across the ridge to Currie and Timber Bowls. While it is possible to hike this trip by going up Currie and Timber Bowls, along the ridge and then down Snake Ridge, it is not recommended as the steep sections are easier and less scary from the other direction.

The two most popular ways of accessing Snake Ridge are via the Cedar Trail at the bottom of the ski runs or taking the chairlift up to the Bear's Den then hiking up to the gun tower at the top of the Bear Run. From the gun tower hike to Snake Ridge across Cedar Bowl. This is a more scenic route than starting at the bottom from Cedar Trail.

Whichever route is taken, the trail up Snake Ridge is marked by a sign (there wasn't one there in 1995 but Linda Socher says there will be in 1996). The trail up Snake Ridge is well-worn and soon after starting up you will come to an area that makes a good stop for views across Cedar Bowl. From this point onward the views improve with each step and red paint markings on the rocks keep you on the route.

Two sections on the Snake Ridge portion of this hike might cause some problems for those who are nervous in exposed places. The first is a roped pitch that must be climbed a short (15 metre) distance past a steep little rock gully. Make sure that only one person at a time uses the rope while the others in your party stand clear. Rocks can inadvertently be dislodged while climbing the rope pitch and cause severe injury to those below.

Further on, towards the top of the ridge there is a second section where a steel cable has been fixed to the rock. The route crosses a small exposed gully and, although there are plenty of handholds plus the security of the cable, caution is in order.

Once on the ridge the route travels southeast through the heather and alpine plants, with uninterrupted views for miles over the Fernie area and beyond. An easy ascent brings you to the top of Griz Peak at 2,070 metres. Continue on and encounter a short traverse along a narrow ridge top that drops away steeply on both sides. A cable fixed to poles placed by the avalanche control team makes a good handrail for anyone who is nervous but this little razorback isn't as bad as some rumours have made it seem. Just don't fall off it.

Ascend to the actual summit of the hike, Polar Peak at 2,100 metres, watching along the way for interesting fossils in the limestone. This must be one of the finest places in the Elk Valley to have lunch, take a nap and consider what really is important in life. It is a place that can make a person feel for a moment like it's a scene from the *Sound of Music*. Members of our party felt compelled to break into poor imitations of Julie Andrews. The magnificence of this site has caused it to become more popular each year and the summit book reflects this. At least fifty parties made it to the top in the 1995 hiking season.

From Polar Peak the trail continues down into Currie Bowl where some parties opt to travel across the boulder field rather than following the trail which loses some elevation before climbing up the other side of the bowl to Timber Bowl. We tried both. The trail takes less time and doesn't require any boulder hopping but the choice is yours.

Once on the ridgetop of Timber Bowl keep an eye open for beargrass along the trail. It is a one to two-metre tall stem topped by a club-like cluster of tiny creamy white blossoms. Please resist the temptation to pick them as the individual plants flower only once per decade.

The final few feet to the top of Snake Ridge

With expansion to the ski resort area in progress some trails are now partly on cat roads. The trail currently follows a cat road for a 100 metres or so to a landing where it again enters the forest on the left.

This descent is a pleasant walk through shady forest, a welcome change on a hot day from the sunny ridges of the earlier parts of the hike. One more brief section of road is encountered before the trail enters the forest at a landing and continues as a trail until intersecting the ski runs for the final descent to the base area of the ski hill.

The entire loop takes a full day of seven to eight hours, depending on the party, rest stops and the time spent enjoying the scenery and wildflowers. Take plenty of water as there is none along the way until the hike is almost over. Also, do not descend from the middle of the ridge at any point. Parties have had to be rescued from the cliffs above the ski runs in the past. Retrace your steps if you run out of time or if weather necessitates a retreat.

Timber Bowl

For half-day hikes in summer heat it's hard to beat this hike, much of which is in the shade. Berry pickers love this moderate five-hour hike up through cool forest and the subalpine beauty of the Timber Bowl.

At the bottom of Currie Bowl take the road south up through Timber Bowl. Spectacular alpine meadows, old growth forests and wildlife viewing opportunities. Mushroom enthusiasts will enjoy this hike in the fall. Timber Bowl is a good option for visitors who don't feel up to the rigours of the High Ridge Traverse or those pressed for time.

Options

There are unlimited routes for the hiker or biker that have not been described here. One of the joys of the ski resort in the summer is endless possibilities. Stand at the bottom, look around and pick a route.

View of Fernie from the Fernie High Ridge Trail

26 Fernie Provincial Park

Easy interpretive walking or mountain-biking trails through the park.

Access: From the south bridge in Fernie travel west 2.3 kilometres then turn right to Fernie Provincial Park.

Park Interpretive Trails

These trails are accessed from the car park or the campground and wind through the park and along Lizard Creek.

The Stove Trail

Route Checkers: Tom Soles & Darcy Richardson

This trail can be hiked but is best done as a mountain bike trip. It offers single-track biking with a highly technical uphill and a screaming downhill that's fun, fun, fun!

Once into the park take the first right, following the campsites to the park garage on your right. At the end of the pavement you will see a cart track heading off to the right, a single track straight ahead (Dem Bones) and a cart track to your left that is blocked with stumps and trees.

Follow the cart track to your left over the blockage to a single track heading into the trees. At the old stove turn right and start climbing to the powerline road. This is a demanding ride, granny gear the entire way up with some highly technical riding. Wet and muddy sections can be expected along the way to the powerline load. Turn right on the powerline road. Once the road levels out watch for a single-track trail to the right which is Dem Bones. If you go straight instead of turning off you can get to the trail up the Moccasin on Mt. Fernie.

Dem Bones

If you choose to turn down onto Dem Bones from the powerline road hold on tight and enjoy one of the best single track downhill rides in the valley. Dem Bones ends up back where you started in the park.

Gorby Trail

Route Checker: Darcy Richardson

This strenuous bike trip is fun and offers great views. The route connects Cedar Valley Road to the Fernie Snow Valley Ski Resort so you can stop there for refreshments. From Fernie Provincial Park continue to the end of the pavement. Here the gravel Cedar Valley Road starts. Travel this road a short distance to a corral on the left hand side just before a cattleguard. Park here to begin the bike trip. Cross the creek and take the left fork to the fence. Cross over the fence and take the right fork. The left fork takes you on a single track through Sherwoody Forest and back around to the park.

The trail is on a cart track which takes you through dense forest to the edge of Gorby Bowl. Follow the cart track across the bowl then down crossing under the Haul Back. The cart track continues down a short distance before leveling off and angling to the right across the ski runs. The cart track crosses under the Boomerang Triple Chair and continues its descent still angling to the right. The cart track crosses under El Quad chair lift and then continues down to the base of the ski hill. You can get back to the park via a trail known to locals as Galloway's Trail. The easiest access for this trail is to ride down to Highway 3 from the ski hill and head back towards Fernie. Just before the first bridge crossing on Highway 3 Galloway's Trail heads off the Highway to your left. Galloway's Trail ends on the road just before the park. Ride back through the park and to your vehicle.

27 Hartley Lake Road

Numerous options with fantastic views and wildlife, wildflower meadows.

Hartley Lake Road is best driven as an access for other trails or family hiking in the meadows along Olivia Creek. As a mountain bike trip it is 10 kilometres of moderate, continuous uphill on packed dirt.

Access: Travel east of the north bridge in Fernie 5.2 kilometres to Dicken Road. Turn left onto Dicken Road and take the first right turn (300 metres) onto the road marked by a sign to Hartley Lake. The road climbs up past a farm and eventually reaches the lake.

Hartley Lake/Sulphur Creek/Bull River

This entire circuit takes a long day - 10 hours on bike. From Dicken Road ride to Hartley Lake (8.5 kilometres) and just beyond to Hartley Pass where the descent begins into the Bull River drainage. About 10 or 11 kilometres down you reach the Sulphur Creek Mineral Lick locally known as the 'stinkhole'. Great wildlife viewing opportunities exist here. In spring and early summer the mountain goat nannies bring their babies down to the lick. Their antics provide marvelous entertainment as they nimbly scamper across the steep cliff face. Deer, elk, bear, moose and other animals also frequent the area which is at the base of a steep face on the left between the second and third bridge across Sulphur Creek.

There is a scenic B.C. Forest Service Recreation campsite just west of the mineral lick. Ride two more kilometres past the campsite to an intersection with the Bull River Road. Turn left traveling south along the Bull River, take the right fork after the dam and cross the canyon and continue to the paved highway. Three more kilometres south brings you to the Bull River Inn, a good place for a shuttle pick-up. Inside, historic photos and artifacts illustrate the colourful past of the Bull River area. Some hardy souls do the loop all the way back to Fernie but it's a long bike ride.

Mt. Hosmer

Route Checkers: Glenn Davis & Debbie Wilson

On clear days from spring through fall a large shadow appears on the massive south face of Mt. Hosmer. As the day wanes the shadow becomes more pronounced and locals refer to it as the Ghostrider. To even the less imaginative it presents an image of a horse coming toward the viewer and depending on who you talk to, the rider is either an Indian maiden, the father of the maiden, a warrior, or William Fernie. The shape to the right of the horse is either William Fernie, the Indian maiden, or the father - apparently real warriors don't walk.

The legend of the Ghostrider states that William Fernie came to the area prospecting. Local natives wore black beads that Fernie recognized as coal. The natives traded the

The Ghostrider appears late in the day on Mt. Hosmer

secret location of the coal for Fernie's promise to marry the chief's daughter. When Fernie reneged on the deal the natives responded by placing a curse on the valley. After the curse the valley was beset with fires, floods and mining disasters which continued until the curse was lifted in a special ceremony in 1964. The shadow remains as a reminder of William Fernie's treachery and the curse.

Seven kilometres up Hartley Lake Road there is a well-marked trailhead for the hike up Mt. Hosmer. This is a moderate five to six-hour hike from the trailhead to the summit and back. From the trailhead to Ghostrider Peak on Mt. Hosmer is 3.5 kilometres with a 900 metre elevation gain.

This is one of the few hikes around Fernie that can legitimately be called a hiking trail. Trail crews have done a fabulous job building the trailhead parking area, grading the route, even providing railings at appropriate viewpoints.

Excellent views all along the way expose the scenic beauty of the Fernie area. A tremendous variety of wildflowers brighten trail sides and creek meadows, even in early September.

Start early on hot days even in the fall as the route up bakes in the sun after 9 or 10 am. Take plenty of water as there is none enroute. After two to three hours of steady uphill hiking a scenic flat area is reached that is perfect for a rest stop and the end of the hike for many. This area is referred to by locals as the saddle - a wonderful lookout with great views of Fernie.

While many people look up to the summit from the lookout and decide to go back down the trail, those who continue on reap far greater rewards. The top isn't as far beyond the saddle as it appears to be and the route is quite enjoyable. It winds past mountain heather, huckleberries and quantities of the tiny delicious grouseberries.

In the bowl on the far side of the summit ridge you might catch a glimpse of a mountain goat. The summit itself (Ghostrider Peak 2,340 metres) is a great place to have lunch and enjoy the spectacular panoramic views of mountains on all sides. The last five-minute leg to the summit is steep so stay away from the edge and watch your step.

View of Elk Valley from the lookout on the saddle

The trip down is a real knee burner but overall this is one of the 'must-do' trips in the Fernie area.

Three Sisters

Route Checkers: Paul Sentes, Gordon & Arthur Sombrowski

The Three Sisters is the dominant mountain feature of the Fernie area, not quite looming-over, but certainly commanding the northwest skyline. It is one of the first mountains to receive the morning light and one of the last to lose it in the evening.

To reach the summit requires a challenging high elevation hike. Traveling through old growth forest and through alpine meadow areas it offers close-up views of the multiple headwaters of Olivia Creek, the Three Sisters cliffs and limestone karst topography. In early summer you may have to cross snowpack to gain access to the ridge near the summit. Wear sturdy footwear and be equipped to deal with changing mountain weather. This is a full-day excursion taking three to five hours to reach the summit.

Travel nine kilometres from the beginning of Hartley Lake Road to the first left turn past Hartley Lake. You enter a cart track which is four-wheel-drive accessible for three kilometres south before coming to an abrupt end. The trail starts here and approaches Three Sisters from the back.

The trail is clearly visible and leads through a heavily wooded section opening up to a small, pretty meadow. Cross the meadow, head west and look for red triangles on the trees. If you don't see them you're not on the trail. The trail is clear and well worn. At first the ascent is steep and can be slippery when wet. Thereafter the trail continues gradually upward into open alpine terrain. The trail fades at points in the alpine terrain so watch for markers such as rock cairns, orange ribbon or triangles on trees. Keep in mind you are walking counter-clockwise around the mountain. Generally stay on the left slope of the mountain except when approaching the saddle. When approaching the saddle go up the middle.

Three Sisters as seen from Fernie

After you go over the saddle you begin to see the Elk Valley and the Ski Resort. Again keep left and aim for the top of the ridge half way to the rock outcrops. This portion of the hike is very steep on a scree slope. Watch your footing in this area until you gain the west ridge of the second sister. Once on the top of the ridge it's a short five minutes to the summit of the middle sister. There is a cairn and a transmitter at the summit. This is one of the highest points in the area at 2,744 metres.

Views stretching in all directions spanning a hundred miles are well worth the effort of reaching the summit. Crowsnest Mountain in Alberta, Fisher Peak, Lake Koocanusa, Fernie and beyond are clearly visible.

Three Sisters Meadow

Follow directions for Three Sisters to the meadow area for great family hiking or picnicking. This meadow is called Camp Four, once the highest of four logging camps numbered from the bottom of Hartley Lake Road. It was also prime area for hunting goats. Last year Sam Caravetta (who has provided a wealth of trivia from the good old days) was chased by a cow moose with a yearling calf in this meadow. From Camp Four there used to be a common hiking and hunting route through the pass dividing Three Sisters from Mt. Proctor and down Fairy Creek. The area up in the pass was known locally as the Black Dirt. You may notice the big headwall to the right known locally as the Soda Wall, typical of the many awesome rock formations in the area.

28 Bear Chutes/Fernie Ridge

Incredible views, spectacular wildflower displays, easy to moderate two-hour uphill hike.

Bear Chutes is a prominent knoll directly across the valley from the Three Sisters. Formerly known as Letcher's Ridge, it is separated from Fernie Ridge by a low area once known as Cratchie's Hollow. It was one of the prime berry picking places for Fernie folks about 50 years ago.

Access: From Fernie take the Coal Creek Road to the first turnoff to the left past the landfill. The road goes uphill a short distance to a gate blocking further access. Park to the left in the clearing where you will have commanding views of the landfill.

The common Elk Valley arnica

Bear Chutes

The trailhead to Bear Chutes is on the old dirt road heading uphill directly across the road from the parking clearing. Follow the road to the top, where the road ends. About half way up the old dirt road crosses a forestry road and continues uphill.

Fine views of Fernie from Bear Chutes

There are many vantage points for views of Fernie along the way so hikers have an excuse to stop whenever they want. However, the best views of the Lizard Range, Fernie and the eastern Elk Valley are at the top where the old road ends. The entire trail is bordered by wildflowers of every variety. In spring and early summer watch for birds in the conifers along the way, especially Pine Grosbeaks. They are robin-sized red birds with rich warbling songs.

As a mountain bike trip it's steep, unrelenting, rough but technically easy. As a hike it's a moderate two-hour uphill climb.

Fernie Ridge

Route Checkers: Pat Gilmar, Jack McKay & David Rafuse

From the top of Bear Chutes you can continue up to Fernie Ridge on foot with some routefinding. Stay to the right of the cliffs and make your way to the top as a final destination or the beginning of the ridge walk to Hosmer. The ridge-walk is probably best done from the Hosmer end however, as the top of the ridge is easier to access from that end. To start from the Hosmer end travel east 10.2 kilometres on Highway 3 from the Fernie north bridge to the Hosmer bridge. From here it's 300 metres to the first turnoff to the right.

Travel 900 metres, crossing the railway tracks then turn right up to the coke oven ruins. Follow the powerline road south for five kilometres to a gate. Park here. Hike back from the gate 300 metres where you will find the trail heading up to the ridge.

The trail is an old four-wheel-drive road that climbs 300 vertical metres to the crest of the ridge. Just before the crest of the ridge leave the road, which continues to the south, and find your way to the ridgetop. You will be in scattered forest for the first 200 meters before it opens up to alpine terrain with beautiful meadows overlooking the Flathead in the distance. There are good views in all directions from the 2,240 metre summit.

The ridge is easy to follow all the way to the top of the Bear Chutes. Descend Bear Chutes to the landfill and your shuttle vehicle, or if you didn't shuttle a vehicle, the problem of getting back to where you started near Hosmer.

29 Coal Creek

Numerous options for hiking and biking.

Access: From Fernie turn on the first right between the railway tracks and Fas Gas onto Pine Ave. Take the first left onto Coal Creek Road. Most of the trailheads in this area are accessed from this road or from Fas Gas.

Eric's Trail/Sidewinder

Route Checker: Terry Goddard

This is a continuous uphill grind, past a trapper's cabin then a short downhill to a logging road. Demanding physically but technically intermediate, Eric's Trail begins off the first road left (Ridgemont Road) past the landfill. Go up this road to a locked yellow gate barring motorized vehicles. The trail begins on the right 20 metres past the yellow gate.

It starts out steep, shrubby and hard packed. There is plenty of uphill with some level spots which are just teasers. You're on the right track if you pass an old trapper's cabin. The trail returns to Ridgemont Road after a short downhill. Overall this is a strenuous two-hour ride. Make sure the granny gear works.

Where Eric's Trail returns to Ridgemont Road you can cross the road and continue down on Sidewinder to 13th. Avenue. Or turn right on Ridgemont Road and follow it a short distance and take Deadfall Trail which is between the two forks in the road down to the Hosmer Powerline Road.

Deadfall Trail

Route Checker: Darcy Richardson

Those seeking variety will enjoy this moderate two to four-hour mountain bike trip. This trip is not technically difficult but you need to be physically fit for the uphills. Narrow, twisting, rooted, rutted, stumpy, swampy, that's the description from the local bikers! You'll also find beautiful views of the valley, orchids in early summer, huckleberries later, and in fall - golden larch trees.

From downtown 2nd Avenue in Fernie cross the railway tracks and ride up the hill taking the first right past Fas Gas. Bike into the very top corner of the cemetery and continue on the road past the fenced water reservoir to a single-track climb that winds up through a cut block. Turn left after a little bridge and ride to the top of the cut block. From here the views of the ski hill and Fernie are excellent.

At the top of the cut block the single track comes out on Ridgemont Road. Turn left on Ridgemont Road and follow it up past the Sidewinder Trail on the left and Eric's Trail on the right. Just after these two trails the road forks. Deadfall Trail is a single track heading straight into the woods between the two forks.

Deadfall Trail continues to climb a short distance then becomes a fast, narrow single-track downhill on the other side to the Hosmer Powerline Road. The trail down has roots, ruts and swampy sections.

Once on the powerline turn left and climb up the hill. Watch for a single-track trail heading down to the right. This trail takes you across the railway tracks to a fence. Cross the fence and ride parallel to the railway tracks toward town for 180 metres. Keep on the lookout for a trail on the right which takes you around the golf course to the Fairgrounds Road and back to town.

A second option once down on the powerline from Deadfall is to take the powerline road to Hosmer. This trip entails a lot of up and down, about 10 kilometres on a grassy, hard-packed trail. Refreshments waiting at Hosmer City Hall keep you motivated. Go left to Hosmer after the coke ovens and ruins of the Hosmer mine. Travel back to Fernie on Highway 3. (That's to the left after you leave City Hall.) A good option on the return is to take Dicken Road

Mountain biker runs over photographer

loop to get off Highway 3. Pack a lunch or snacks and plenty of water.

Educational Forest Trails

Route Checkers: Rob & Matthew Morrison, Evan & Scott Davis, Matthew Wright

This pleasant area features a system of trails and interpretive signs through a variety of ecosystems featuring over 700 species of plants. Wildlife and a variety of birds can be found throughout the trail system. This can be a fun evening bike ride or a leisurely afternoon family stroll.

Follow Coal Creek Road until the pavement ends and take the first right. Cross the bridge to the trail sign immediately on the left hand side. If you see people standing on their heads trying to figure out the trail map signs you are in the right place. The trails are easy but fun for biking. Open fields of daisies and purple vetch are interspersed with shady sections through the forest.

Roots Trail

Route Checker: Darcy Richardson

The most popular single-track ride in Fernie, it has a short uphill climb, fun-filled, twisting and technical downhills and takes less than one hour via the Nature Trails loop.

Take Coal Creek Road heading toward the landfill. Turn on the first right past the end of the pavement. Cross the bridge and the trailhead for the Educational Forest is to the left.

Once at the trailhead follow the nature trails keeping to the right and you'll end up on the powerline behind the trailer court. Keep following the powerline to where it turns left and makes a short climb to River Road Extension.

On River Road Extension turn right and ride 50 meters around the corner and look left to see the beginning of Roots (a single-track trail heading uphill). The trail starts climbing immediately and you'll find out soon enough why it's called Roots.

Climbing past an old log cabin the trail heads right and reveals one of the best views of the ski hill in the whole valley. Still ascending, the trail crosses Ridgemont Road then, just before the down-hill action begins, there's one steep little climb with a crazy little root at the top. At the pitch on the top try the old front wheel lift and back tire lunge popping right over the crazy root, (it works well in theory if you make excellent effort, if not - well that's why we love our sport; the challenge - there's always next time).

After the crazy root the trail levels out at a log-pile ramp (go around; going over hurts). Now the fun begins with a fast and twisty downhill back to River Road Extension. Once on the road go right down to the rock cairn on the left hand side of the road and back down into the nature trails following them back to the bridge, completing the loop.

La Bamba

Route Checkers: Judy McMahon & Heinz Weixelbaum

This is a short five-minute route connecting River Road Extension and Cokato Road. From Fas Gas travel 3.7 kilometres on Cokato Road. The trail is located on the left side of Cokato Road.

Coal Creek Historical Trail

Route Checker: Pat Gilmar

Almost a reality, this trail was being developed at the time of writing this book. By the spring of 1996 signage should be complete. There will be a trail and historical description sign on Second Avenue, an interpretive sign at the viewpoint just beyond the gun range, and the trail will be tagged the whole way. Crestbrook Forest Industries will be putting in two bridges.

Behind the Fas Gas service station take the trail east and follow the old railway grade which runs parallel to Coal Creek and the Coal Creek Road. Continue past the landfill

Mountain biker above Coal Creek Road. Ski Hill in the background.

to Ridgemont Road and turn left then immediately right. Follow this old road grade to Coal Creek Road, go around the gun range then take the first trail to the left onto the old road again. It's about three hours to the old townsite and back. The perfect family outing on bikes.

Morrissey Ridge Walk

Anyone who has noticed the microwave tower on the ridge southeast of Fernie must have wondered about the view from there. Although most people drive to the viewpoint, there is good hiking along the ridgetop offering great views and berry picking along the way.

Take the Coal Creek Road about 9 to 10 kilometres (from Fas Gas) to the turnoff to your right onto Matheson Creek Road opposite the tin sheds. This takes you to the BC Tel Microwave Communications Tower and the easiest-accessed high views of the valley. A four-wheel-drive vehicle or mountain bike is required to access the tower area.

From the summit of Morrissey Ridge walk along the crest enjoying great views and alpine meadows. For an extended hike traverse south and drop into Morrissey Creek Valley. No established trail exists so routefinding skills are required.

Castle Mountain

Route Checkers: Judy McMahon & Heinz Weixelbaum

Castle Mountain is the big bump on the north end of Morrissey Ridge, its cliff bands reminiscent of castle walls. It requires a moderate four-hour hike from Upper River Road Extension.

Take Coal Creek Road turning right on the Upper River Road Extension. Access is from logging roads and powerline roads leading east off Upper River Road Extension. Apparently it requires routefinding skills as the route is mostly following game trails. Rumour has it that the forest is predominantly lodgepole pine and so the understory is not too thick. Hopefully the rumour isn't too thick. Once on top you find a grassy slope with a rock cairn, a bottle for writing comments, and a great view.

At the time of writing this book the local bikers were developing a trail from Roots called "Hyper Extension". This trail currently takes you about 2/3 the way up Castle Mountain. By the summer of '96 it could go the entire way.

Coal Creek/Flathead/Lodgepole/Morrissey Loop

This route is most definitely best done as an overnight trip since it is a 120-kilometre bike loop. It offers plenty of wildlife viewing opportunities along different creeks around the loop. Fall is a great time for this trip, featuring spectacular colours along the mountain slopes.

From Fernie Fas Gas take the Coal Creek Road for a steady climb to Coal Creek Pass. About 10 kilometres up you'll encounter tin sheds on your left opposite Matheson Creek Road which is the turnoff for the Microwave Tower on Morrissey Ridge. Stay on Coal Creek Road.

After the tin sheds the road levels out winding through the valley to the pass at about kilometre 18. From the pass it is a downhill ride to a creek crossing (bridge might be there).

The road winds up and down from the crossing to a cattleguard and a fork in the road. Take the right fork across another creek (bridge might be there) and within two kilometres you are connected with the Corbin Creek Road. From Fas Gas to Corbin Creek Road is approximately 31 kilometres.

Turn right on Corbin Creek Road and travel about 21 kilometres to the Fording Mine. This section is well traveled with traffic from the mine so care is advised. Once at the mine the Flathead Road continues to your right across a small creek. The road skirts the mining property on its left. From the mine it is a steady climb for about nine kilometres to Flathead Pass.

After the pass it's a fun ride, winding down to the valley floor and along the valley with mountains on either side. From the pass it's approximately 10 kilometres to a fork in the road.

Take the right fork following McLatchie Creek Road, crossing a bridge and heading uphill. You'll encounter a small lake on your right with an outfitter's cabin a short distance up. There is a good chance of seeing moose along this section. The road winds uphill with a shallow grade and then a fun, fast downhill on the other side to the intersection with Lodgepole Road. From the McLatchie Creek Road it is approximately 15 kilometres to the intersection with Lodgepole Road just west of Harvey Pass.

Turn right on Lodgepole Road following Lodgepole Creek as it winds through the valley. Continue to your right at the Ram Creek Road intersection. There is a great five kilometre downhill ride to the intersection of River Road on your left. Continue past the intersection staying on Lodgepole Road to the stop sign. The road to your right is Morrissey Road, the road straight ahead is the River Road Extension and the road to your left (the one you want to take) is Morrissey Road. From Lodgepole Road to the stop sign is about 26 kilometres.

From the stop sign it is three kilometres to the intersection with Cokato Road and the turnoff to the bridge across the Elk River and Highway 3. From the intersection to Fas Gas via Cokato Road is 14.7 kilometres.

30 Cokato Road

Many options that are best for mountain biking.

Access: Take the first right (Pine Avenue) between the railway tracks and Fas Gas. This eventually becomes Cokato Road. The pavement ends 5.5 kilometres from Fas Gas. Most trips in this section are accessed from Cokato Road.

Morrissey/Lodgepole/Flathead/Bighorn Creek

Those wanting a bike loop in the Flathead area with a few more options can try this 170-kilometre (approximately) loop. Camping is available about halfway at the Butts Forestry Recreation Site at the junction of Border Road and Flathead Road. Travel 14.7 kilometres on Cokato Road. From this point the road continues straight ahead as Morrissey Road. Take Morrissey Road west for three kilometres to a fork, then take the right fork onto Lodgepole Road. From the fork it is about 9.2 kilometres (including a 5-kilometre climb) to the Lodgepole - Ram Creek Road intersection. Turn left, staying on Lodgepole Road and continue 17.7 kilometres as the road winds through the valley following Lodgepole Creek to the intersection with McLatchie Creek Road. Stay on Lodgepole Road and climb over Harvey Pass to the intersection with Flathead Road, a distance of approximately 15 kilometres.

Turn right on the Flathead Road and continue to the intersection with Border Road approximately 16.5 kilometres further. Turn right (west) on Border Road following it about three kilometres and take the right fork on Cabin/Ram Road. It is approximately 63.5 kilometres from the beginning of Cabin/Ram Road to complete the loop at the intersection with Lodgepole Road.

At the confluence of Bighorn Creek, (Ram Creek,) and the Wigwam River is a Forestry Campsite. (Snowshoe Lake is accessible from here.) You will begin seeing Mt. Broadwood and the China Wall as you reach the top of the climb out of the valley. Another three kilometres and you have completed the loop at the intersection of Lodgepole Road and Ram Creek Road. Continue back to Fas Gas from here.

Snowshoe Lake

The trail to Snowshoe Lake starts from the campsite at the confluence of the Wigwam River and Bighorn Creek. Follow the directions above to the campsite at the confluence of Bighorn Creek and the Wigwam River. From the campsite follow the cart track across Bighorn Creek 2.5 kilometres to the trail on your right leading down to the

Wigwam River. Wade the river to the trailhead and hike the one kilometre to Snowshoe Lake. (This trip is best done in late summer when the Wigwam River is low enough to wade.)

Cart Track Extension

Route Checker: Pat Gilmar

The second option from the Forestry Campsite is to continue along the cart track approximately 20 kilometres to the end of the cart track. Here a single-track mountain bike trail continues for four kilometres. At its end turn around and come back the way you came.

Wigwam Flats

Route Checker: Pat Gilmar

The largest donation of it's kind in Canadian history, this 22,102 acre conservancy was donated by Shell Canada Ltd. to the Nature Conservancy of Canada. This area is critical habitat for many big game species such as: Rocky Mountain bighorn sheep, elk, white tail deer, cougar, black and grizzly bear.

When viewing or photographing wildlife maintain a safe distance and keep noise down so as not to disturb their natural patterns. The best wildlife viewing opportunities are in April and May.

Requiring a half day for strong bikers and a full day for most, Mt. Broadwood Nature Conservancy, locally known as Wigwam Flats, can be accessed from two locations.

To access the Wigwam Flats from the west turn off Highway 3 at Morrissey Provincial Park located 14 kilometres east of the north bridge in Fernie. Follow the road past the park and cross the bridge over the Elk River. Cross the railway tracks and turn right onto Morrissey Road. Travel three kilometres and take the right fork onto Lodgepole Road. Follow Lodgepole Road 9.2 kilometres to where the road forks. Turn right onto the Ram Creek Road and follow this road three kilometres to the road on your right to Wigwam Flats. Turn right onto this road and drive to the locked gate and park.

The east access, which is easiest and the one we recommend, departs from Elko. At Elko take the first left off Highway 3 south of the railway overpass. Follow Main Street and turn right on Alexander Ave. Take the first gravel road (River Road) to the left down to the bridge across the Elk River. Immediately turn right after crossing the bridge and park your vehicle. The gate on this road is locked and closed to vehicle traffic except June 15 to July 15.

Follow the road past the locked gate along the Elk River Canyon to an old apple orchard on the left side of the road. From here it is possible to continue straight down to the Wigwam River, however, the recommended route is to turn left at the orchard. Follow this road taking the right fork to avoid a very steep hill. This brings you along a ridge with the Wigwam below.

The road along the ridge hugs the base of Mt. Broadwood, a spectacular geographic feature. Once on the flats you can stay on the road or follow game trails. Return to your vehicle the way you came.

Morrissey Falls

This trip is great for an afternoon bike ride. Follow Cokato road 14 kilometres to where it continues as Morrissey Road. Stay on Morrissey Road 11.3 kilometres.

Just before the falls the road runs parallel to the Hydro line overhead and encounters a hairpin turn. The road will then leave the hydro line and this is the point to begin listening for the falls as they are not visible from the road. They are on the left side down a very steep embankment. Further up the road are other falls that can be observed from the road.

31 Silver Springs Lake

Easy 10-minute hike to a wonderful lake surrounded by steep cliffs with options to a second and third lake.

Route Checker: Jack Mckay & Glenn Davis

Silver Springs Lake is almost too accessible. It's only a 10 minute hike and because of this is starting to suffer from 'yahoo syndrome'. Popular with local youths who dive off the cliffs into the clear emerald waters, it can get intrusively loud and partyish on a hot summer day. The preferred times to go are in early spring or in late fall when it's much quieter.

This is a premier area for spring flower enthusiasts. In May when the alpine meadows are still under snow, the lake area is already bright with flowers. A short walk along the lakes reveals colourful wild gardens of Columbia virgin's

Tranquillity at Silver Springs Lake is found in spring & fall
Photo Credit - Judy McMahon

bower, yellow fawn lily, Calypso orchids, shooting stars, forget-me-nots, and Indian paintbrush. By midsummer the mix changes to Indian paintbrush, fireweed, spotted saxifrage, larkspurs and Queen's cup. Berries such as Saskatoons, wild raspberries, and huckleberries are abundant in late summer and early fall. There is also good wildlife viewing, especially at the upper lakes. Mountain sheep, deer, woodpeckers, loons, and goldeneyes, inhabit the area. When not crowded Silver Springs is a fabulous area for naturalists.

Access: At Elko take the first left off Highway 3 south of the railway overpass. Follow Main Street and turn right on Alexander Ave. Take the first gravel road (River Road) to the left down to the bridge across the Elk River Reservoir.

Those wishing to access Silver Springs Lakes via mountain bike can take the first road to the right immediately after crossing the bridge over the Elk River Reservoir. There is a gate here closing the road to motorized vehicles. Park here and bike the road past the gate to the first left on a trail which goes up to the first lake. It takes about 30 minutes with quite a bit of climbing.

Those driving continue on River Road after crossing the bridge three kilometres to the first dirt road to the right. Turn on this road and follow it west up the powerline to a gate and parking area.

Route: From the parking area a rough four-wheel drive road heads south uphill. An easy 10 minute uphill hike on this road brings you to the first lake. You can hike a loop around the first two lakes or continue to the third lake. Give yourself about two hours for either option.

32 Kikomun Creek

An easy one to two-hour stroll around three lakes to enjoy the turtles, birds and wildflowers.

Kikomun Creek Provincial Park is the largest low elevation park in the East Kootenays. Within its 619 hectares lives a wide variety of plant, animal and bird life. Most unusual is the large natural population of western painted turtles. Natural predators of the young include coyotes, badgers and great blue herons. Turtles are a special feature of this park and are a protected species. It is an offense to abuse turtles or remove them from the park.

Emerald-green Surveyor's Lake is the most accessible and the largest of the three. An Osprey nest close to the picnic tables and sandy swimming beach adds to the lake's appeal. Saunder Lake is connected to Surveyor's Lake by a small stream. There is a footbridge over the stream connecting the two lakes. This footbridge is the best place to view Saunder Lake as there is no hiking trail around this lake. Hidden Lake is not visible from Surveyor's Lake and requires hiking a trail through the forest and the campground to reach it. Hidden Lake is the most secluded of the three lakes, something enjoyed by the infrequent visitors to the lake and the painted turtles who reside there.

All three lakes are bordered with wildflowers which bloom as early as May 1. Oregon grape, pink phlox, brown-eyed susan, gromwell and shooting stars are just a few. Bird watchers can see a variety of small birds such as chickadees, belted kingfishers, dark-eyed juncos, nuthatches, flickers and bluebirds. Common loons, osprey, common goldeneyes, and mallards make the lakes their summer home. Animal life is varied with elk, deer and black bears, as well as smaller mammals such as chipmunks, porcupines and beavers frequenting the area.

Access: From Elko there are two possible routes to Kikomun Creek Provincial Park. For the first route travel west five kilometres to the '93 South junction. Go south 9.8 kilometres to the Jaffray/Baynes Lake turnoff. Take this road west 7.7 kilometres to Kikomun Road. Turn left and travel .5 kilometres to the turnoff into the park. To access the park from the second, easier route, travel west two kilometres past the 93 south junction to the Kikomun-Newgate Road. Turn left and travel 7.2 kilometres to the turnoff into the park. Once inside the park there are signs directing you to day parking at Surveyor's Lake or camping at Surveyor's Lake campground.

Western painted turtles thrive at Hidden Lake

Route: From the second Surveyor's Lake dayparking lot follow the stairs down to the lake. From here you can travel either way around the lake, crossing a wooden foot bridge separating Surveyor and Saunder lakes. To reach Hidden Lake follow the trail around Surveyor's Lake taking the left turn up the hill just before the picnicking area. The trail travels through the camping area to Hidden Lake. Trails are well groomed with gentle slopes around the lakes.

33 Elk River

Numerous put-ins and take-outs from Elkford to Elko.

The Elk River, rising in Elk Lakes Provincial Park runs south, turning west near Sparwood before joining Koocanusa Lake southwest of Elko. From the Elk Lakes the river grows from a shallow, narrow babbling brook to a seriously raging white water river before it enters the Kootenay River south of Elko. During spring runoff the river can become a raging destructive torrent as in the 1995 flood. Later in the summer and during the fall it can be a gentle float trip for families on tubes. It is also a fly fishing Mecca.

Because of the change in water level during the different seasons it is impossible to give a route description like a trail. The put-ins and take-outs however, remain in the same locations season to season.

Most of the rapids that are play waves for kayakers are found in the same sections of the river from season to season although they do change in grade.

Most of the river is mellow and suitable for novice white water paddlers with the exception of one section of river through the canyon which is recommended for expert white water paddlers only. This section on the lower Elk has taught many hard lessons while destroying quite a few nice boats and bruising a lot of egos. Whatever the nature of the water in the section, use your judgment based on your abilities and limits. When in doubt, beach and look ahead for log jams, sweepers, fast channels and shallow channels.

Traveling the river is an excellent way to see the abundant wildlife of the Elk Valley. Watch for dippers, herons, spotted sandpipers, mergansers, geese, and big game.

Round Prairie to Elkford

The put-in at Round Prairie bridge is 5.6 kilometres north of Elkford on Elk Lakes Pass Road. From the put-in it is a short, easy paddle to the take-out at Elkford. The take-out is on your right just before the bridge.

Elkford to Line Creek

Route Checker: Glenn Davis

From the four-way stop in Elkford turn right onto the Fording Mine Road. Turn left just before the bridge to a parking area. The put-in is just down the river bank from here. From the put-in at Elkford to the take-out at the Line Creek bridge is only five kilometres with Grade II water to be expected.

Since the flood in 1995 the river has been changed considerable in this section and we do not recommend paddling it. It now takes about eight hours and is very difficult to navigate in places. We spent a lot of time wading through ooze, dragging our boat through old clearcuts flooded in the spring of 95, and portaging where it was impossible to continue by river. The river channels were braided making it hard to find the proper channel. Log jams spanning the entire river were hidden around bends in the river making it extremely dangerous.

Line Creek to Sparwood Leisure Center

Route Checker: Glenn Davis

Travel north of Sparwood on Highway 43 to the turnoff to the Line Creek Mine on your right. Follow this road across the bridge over the Elk River. Turn to your right once across the bridge and follow the road down to the edge of the river. Line Creek enters the Elk River on the left side of the bridge.

From the put-in at Line Creek to the Sparwood Leisure Center is about 3.5 hours (16 kilometres) with Grade II water. This section of the river is remote and therefore very relaxing and peaceful. Watch for wildlife along the river banks and especially herons fishing in the river. You will encounter some fast water and rapids around Grave Prairie. Kayakers surf these rapids from early to mid-July.

The river travels through Sparwood and under a bridge on Highway 43. Just after going under the bridge Michel Creek enters the Elk River. Once Michel Creek enters watch for the take-out on the left side of the bank. The take-out is directly below the railway crossing and behind the Sparwood Leisure Centre.

The Elk River is a placid stream for most of its length

Sparwood Leisure Center to Garret Ready Mix

Route Checker: Glenn Davis

Turn left off Highway 3 just before the Travel Infocentre in Sparwood onto Red Cedar Drive. Travel this road to its end and turn right on Pine Avenue into the Sparwood Leisure Centre parking lot. The put-in is across the railway tracks and over the bank from the parking lot. From the put-in at the Sparwood Leisure Center to the take-out at Garret Ready Mix is 1.5 hours with Grade II water. This is a gentle paddle with a few surfing waves around the bends in the river when the water levels are high. Just downstream of Garret Ready Mix you will be able to see Highway 3. The river is fairly wide here and you need to stay on the left side of the river to get to the take-out spot which is where the river curves to the right parallel to the highway.

Garret Ready Mix to Hosmer bridge

Route Checker: Glenn Davis

From the north bridge in Fernie travel east on Highway 3, 19.6 kilometres to the turn-off on your left. Take this gravel road across the railway tracks to the parking area on your left. The put-in is down the bank from the parking area. From the put-in just downstream of Garret Ready Mix to the Hosmer Bridge take-out is about 1.5 hours with Grade II water and a few Grade II+ rapids when water levels are high. This section of the river runs parallel to the highway and traffic noise can be heard. You will be able to see the Hosmer bridge from a good distance away. Angle towards the right bank to the take-out just before the bridge.

Hosmer bridge to second Fernie bridge (south bridge)

Route Checkers: Judy McMahon & Heinz Weixelbaum

From the Fernie north bridge travel on Highway 3 nine kilometres to the Hosmer bridge. Turn left on a gravel road just before the bridge and follow this road 75 metres to the put-in at the river's edge. From the put-in at the Hosmer Bridge to the take-out at the south bridge in Fernie is about 1.5 hours with Grade I and II water.

The river in this section has small but thrilling rapids, numerous channels and sweepers to watch for. From the river, Mt. Hosmer, Mt. Proctor and the Lizard Range are all visible. Just after the put-in the river widens considerably and the water becomes quite shallow requiring a bit of navigating through the channels. After this shallow section the river is fairly easy to navigate as long as you look ahead to avoid shallow areas and rapids. The take-out is on the left side of the river just before the second bridge in Fernie.

Fernie south bridge to Morrissey bridge

Route Checkesr: Judy McMahon & Heinz Weixelbaum

From the parking lot at Rip 'N' Richard's in Fernie the put-in is down the bank just upstream from the south bridge. From the put-in at the south bridge to the take-out at the

Morrissey bridge is about a two-hour trip with Grade I and II water. The river runs quite close to Highway 3 so noise from traffic can be heard. This section of the river is a easy float leading through gradual river bends and occasional forks and rapids. About 4 to 5 kilometres from the put-in the river flows fast to the right then makes a sharp, narrow left creating exciting little rapids. This is a fun little rapid even though you may get wet from the spray. You will be able to see the bridge at Morrissey crossing the river from a good distance away. Stay close to the right bank for the take-out immediately after the bridge.

Morrissey bridge to Elko

From the south bridge in Fernie travel west 14 kilometres to a paved road turning off to your left. Follow this road about 600 metres to a dirt road turning off to the right just before the bridge. Turn right on this road and follow it down to the river's edge where you can park. The put-in is here just down river from the bridge. The section from the put-in at Morrissey bridge to Elko is 14 kilometres with Grade I and II water. This section of the river is remote and is a peaceful paddle with wildlife viewing opportunities along the banks of the river. The take-out is on the left bank of the river immediately after the bridge crossing the Elk River Reservoir at Elko. **Extreme Hazard** below the take-out - BC. Hydro Dam!!!

ANG Pipeline Crossing to Highway 93 bridge over the Elk River

Traveling west on Highway 3 turn south onto Highway 93 just past Elko. Follow Highway 93 approximately 2.5 kilometres south taking the first gravel road to your left (east). Follow this gravel road about one kilometre and turn onto the pipeline right-of-way. This right-of-way is private property so please respect the area. Follow the right-of-way taking all the left forks to the parking area for the put-in. From the parking area you follow an old gravel cart track

200 metres down to the put-in on the river. This cart track is difficult to descend as it is covered in loose rock and is quite steep.

From the put-in to the take-out at the bridge crossing on Highway 93 is 10 kilometres with Grade III and IV drops. This section of the river is for expert paddlers only. For those who are not experts the best way to paddle this section is by engaging the services of a professional rafting outfitter.

From the put-in the swift current of the river flows through a spectacular narrow canyon setting. Mountain sheep on the steep walls are commonly seen along this canyon. Rapids and drops are numerous throughout the canyon area with few places to drop your guard until you are clear of the canyon.

Once out of the canyon the river widens with the rapids becoming gentler and further apart. The Wigwam River flows into the Elk River shortly after the canyon and the left bank at the confluence of the two rivers is a good place to stop for lunch. From the confluence of the two rivers to the take-out is the gentlest part of the river allowing you to relax and just float. You will be able to see the bridge over the Elk River on Highway 93 from a good distance. Stay close to the left bank of the river as the take-out is on this side just before the bridge.

To reach the take-out by vehicle travel south on Highway 93 to the bridge crossing the Elk River. Immediately after crossing the bridge turn left on a narrow dirt road leading down to the river.

Wigwam River

The Wigwam River is a nice diversion from paddling the Elk River. From Elko take the first left off Highway 3 south of the railway overpass. Follow Main Street and turn right on Alexander Avenue. Take the first gravel road (River Road) to the left down to the bridge across the Elk River Reservoir. Turn right immediately after the bridge on a dirt

The lower Elk River is for serious paddlers only

road. This road is only open to traffic from June 15 to July 15. Follow this road down to the put-in at the confluence of Lodgepole Creek and the Wigwam River.

The Wigwam River is Grade IV+ and suitable only for experienced paddlers. The river is not suitable for rafts as it is too narrow in places. The Wigwam River is exciting but you need to scout ahead as there can be log jams on the river. The area the river flows through is very scenic and has wildlife viewing potential. The Wigwam flows into the Elk River and becomes a gentle paddle on the Elk River to the take-out just upstream from the bridge crossing Highway 93 and on the left bank of the river.

Resources

Fernie Chamber of Commerce, Hwy. 3 and Dicken Road, Fernie, B.C. V0B 1M0 Phone: 423- 6868

Sparwood Chamber of Commerce, Hwy. 3 and Aspen Drive, Box 1448 Sparwood, B.C. V0B 2G0 Phone: 425-2423

Elkford Chamber of Commerce, 4A Front Street, Box 220 Elkford, B.C. V0B 1H0 Phone: 865-4614

Please note: The area code for all listings is (604) until October 1996 when it will become (250).

ACCOMMODATIONS

Black Nugget Moter Inn 425-2236, 1-800-663-2706 Fax 425-6552 Box 38, Sparwood, B.C., V0B 2G0 Lic. full menu Restaurant & Dining Room

Cedar Lodge Restaurant & Lodge 423-4622 Fax 423-3011 Box 1477, Hwy. 3, Fernie, B.C., V0B 1M0

East Kootenay Mountain View Motel 423-9266 Fax 423-4002, 1302 Hwy. 3 Box 700, Fernie, B.C., V0B 1M0

Elk Island Hotel 865-2211 Fax 865-7844, 808 Michel Rd., Elkford, B.C., V0B 1H0

Fernie Central Reservations 423-9284 Fax 423-4588, 31 Timberline, W. Fernie, B.C., V0B 1M1

Fernie International Hostel & Motel 423-6811 Fax 423-6812, 892 6th Ave., Fernie, B.C., V0B 1M0

Fernie Ski & Summer Resort - Timberline Village Condominiums 423-6878, 1-800-667-9911 Fax 423-7006, 52 Timberline Crescent Box 1316, Fernie, B.C., V0B 1M0

Hi-3 Lodge 423-4492, 1-800-667-1167 Fax 423-6004 Hwy. 3 Box 1230, Fernie, B.C., V0B 1M0

Island Lake Lodge 423-3700 Fax: 423-4055 Cedar Valley Road, Fernie, B.C., V0B 1M1

Koocanusa Campsite & Marina (sum.) 529-7484 (win.) 423-7136 Fax 423-7610 Box 1500, Fernie, B.C., V0B 1M0

Park Place Lodge 423-6871 Fax 423-3773, 742 Hwy. 3 Box 2560, Fernie, B.C., V0B 1M0

Royal Hotel 423-7750, 501 - 1st Ave. Box 1508, Fernie, B.C. V0B 1M0

Crossing Box 426, Blairmore, Alta., T0K 0E0, B & B, Lic. dining, Outdoor hot tub

The Wolf's Den Inn 423-9202 Fax 432-4048 Fernie Ski Hill Accomodation, Ski Area Rd. Fernie, B.C., V0B 1M0

Three Sisters Motel & Lil' Richie's Restaurant 423-4438 Fax 423-6220, 441 Hwy. 3 Box 1349, Fernie, B.C., V0B 1M0

The Inn On The Border 425-0153 Hwy. 3 B.C./Alta. Border

Bed & Breakfasts

Barbara Lynn's Country Inn B & B Ph./ Fax 423-6027, 7th & 7th Box 1077, Fernie, B.C., V0B 1M0

Elk River Chalet B & B 423-7769, 9465 Hwy. 3, W. Fernie, B.C., V0B 1M0 Private baths, Solariums, Located on the river

The Log Inn B & B 423-7524, 25 Anderson Rd., Fernie, B.C., V0B 1M1

Mountainside Inn B & B 423-3754, 50 Timberline Crescent, Fernie, B.C., V0B 1M1 Private baths, Forest secluded hot tub

Wayne's World B & B 423-6320 Box 1113, Fernie, B.C., V0B 1M0

Wild Flower B & B 423-6484, 12 Parkland Drive, Fernie, B.C., V0B 1M0

Recreation & Outfitters

Canyon Raft Company Ltd. 423-7226

Fernie Sports 423-3611 Fax 423-6677 Hwy. 3 Box 1538, Fernie, B.C., V0B 1M0

Ghostrider Sports Ph./Fax 423-4838, 1241 - 7th Ave., Hwy. 3 Box 1767, Fernie, B.C., V0B 1M0

Height of the Rockies Summer Adv., Outfitted by: Elk Valley Bighorn Outfitters Ltd. Ph./Fax 426-5789 Box 275 Cranbrook, B.C., V1C 4H8

Redan Sporting Goods 865-2793 Fax 865-2370, 4A Front St. Box 69, Elkford, B.C., V0B 1H0

S.V. Ski Base 423-6464 Downtown location - 432 - 2nd Ave., Fernie, B.C., V0B 1M0 Ski Hill store outlet during winter months.

The Adventure Shop 423-3515 Fax 423-6556 Specializes in Wildness adventure for fly fishing, Hoseback adv., Wildlife viewing, Mtn. biking

Fernie Golf & Country Club 423-7773 Fax 423-6575 Box 2738, Fernie, B.C., V0B 1M0

Restaurants

Alpine Restuarant 423-3211, 562 - 7th Ave., Hwy. 3, Fernie

Country Tyme Natural Foods & Cafe 423-6580, 692 - 2nd Ave., Fernie

Gabriella's Pasta Place 423-7388, 301 - 2nd Ave., Fernie

Ginger Beef Chinese Restaurant 423-4611, 551 - 2nd Ave., Fernie

Grandma's Place 423-4482 Hwy. 3, Fernie

Hot Spot Family Restaurant 425-6996, 74 - 101 Red Cedar Drive, Sparwood

JV's Pantry, Johnny's Fine Dining 423-3848, 702 - 2nd Ave., Fernie

Libby's Family Restaurant & Pizza 423-7444 or 423-7711 Hwy. 3, Fernie

Our Cappuccino Corner 423-4224, 502 - 2nd Ave., Fernie

Rip & Richard's Eatery 423-3002 Fax 423-3782, 301 Hwy. 3, Fernie

Smitty's Family Rest., Husky Gas Bar 423-3892 Hwy. 3, Fernie

The Old Elevator 423-7115, 291 - 1st Ave., Fernie

Zacharia's Greek & Italian Cuisine 425-4400, 104 Centenial Square, Sparwood